Flying Start

Flying Start

by

Jo Gardiner

First published in 1999 by
The Industrial Society
Robert Hyde House
48 Bryanston Square
London W1H 7LN

© The Industrial Society 1999

ISBN 1 85835 587 7

Stylus Publishing Inc.
22883 Quicksilver Drive
Sterling
VA 20166-2012
USA

British Library Cataloguing-in-Publication Data.
A catalogue record for this book is available from the
British Library.

Typeset by: Midlands Book Typesetting
Printed by: The Cromwell Press
Cover by: Sign Design
Cover illustration by: Paul Vismara/SIS

The Industrial Society is a Registered Charity No. 290003

Acknowledgements

Thanks to all the colleagues – experts in their fields – whose advice I have incorporated into this book. They include Debra Allcock, Alan Barker, Andrew Forrest and Judi James. Their books are listed in Part Seven, and I'd recommend them if you want to go into specific areas in more detail.

Thanks also to the following colleagues who are such great role models: Julie Amber, Dipti Bhatt, Tony Bolton, Joy Buchan, Mag Connolly, Maria Darnell, Jenny Davenport, Debbie Greest, Gill Hyatt, Suzanne Hyde, Angela Ishmael, Anji Jani, Paul Johnson, John Knell, Deborah Layde, Brendan McDonagh, Pat McGuinness, Louise Mackie, Roger Opie, Gill Sargeant, Grace Tasker and Chrissie Wright.

Thanks too to Henry Scrope and Pat Bellamy for their advice on employment law.

Finally, many thanks to Jessica Bone, Liz Cook, Sam Mabb and Stefan Stern for their friendship, love and support – at work and after hours.

Contents

Introduction

Most of us start our first 'proper' job without any idea of what
working life is really like. Some organizations are great – they
help new people settle in and find out what they need to know.
Other employers just expect you to find your own way – almost
seeing it as a test (if you can find your own way round and sort
yourself out, then you're worth employing). The workplace
has its own rules – some written, many unwritten – and it can
be tough at times for all sorts of reasons. But working life
should be a fair deal – you put something in (your time, skills,
effort, enthusiasm) and you get something out (pay,
opportunities to learn and develop skills, a sense of achievement,
good company). For many people, paid work is a vital part of
life, giving financial independence, and a sense of identity and
direction. We all learn the tricks of the trade as we progress
through our working lives, but it usually helps to understand
things about work and working life sooner rather than later.
Which is what this book is about.

**Flying Start aims to explain the key things you need to
know about work and jobs**. It covers practical, everyday issues,
suggests how to handle problems, and explains some of the things
you'll come across in a lot of workplaces.

This book doesn't aim to go into any issue in great detail (this
is supposed to be a handy guide, not an encyclopaedia) but it does

suggest where to go for more information or help on specific issues.

Flying Start is aimed at anyone in (or hoping to get in to) their first 'proper' job – or their first job after a long time away from the workplace (during which time many things may have changed). You may want to read most or all of it, just to get a broad picture of the kinds of issues that crop up, or you could dip into various sections, depending on your day-to-day needs.

Above all, this book is designed to give you a bit of confidence in yourself. You've got the job – which is great – and you're on the first rung of the work ladder. *Flying Start* will help you feel a bit more confident as you hang onto and climb that ladder. Good luck!

Part One

Starting a job

Starting a job

Getting a job is never easy, and sometimes it's very difficult. You've probably:

- looked for vacancies (either ones you've spotted yourself or ones the Employment or Careers Service have picked out for you)
- filled in application forms
- gone for interviews
- taken tests
- waited (for what seems like ages!)

You may have been lucky and got one of the first jobs you applied for, or you may have applied many times before finally getting a job. You may be starting a job you're really keen on – the kind of job you wanted to get – or you may have ended up in the kind of job that doesn't really match up to what you wanted to do, or you may have changed your mind and realized you wanted to do something different. You may see this job as the first stage in a planned career, or you may have taken the job mainly to earn some money and be in work. You may even have been told to take the job – as part of an Employment Service programme.

So you may be starting with high hopes – or without much enthusiasm. However you feel, it's important to look at this job as an opportunity to learn. You'll be part of a team, taking on new responsibilities and developing new skills. Sometimes you'll have bad days, weeks, even months – but your job's an opportunity, the first rung on the ladder.

You may already have some work experience – from a Saturday job, holiday job or work placement as part of a course at school or college, or from previous full-time employment. You'll probably find some of that experience useful (timekeeping, working as a team member, dealing with customers, etc.) but there will probably be loads of new things to get to grips with. It's OK to be new, to have to ask, to feel a bit lost when everyone else looks like an expert! Remember that they were once new too – and while you've got a lot to learn you have your own mix of skills and abilities and you can make a valuable contribution.

If things don't work out – you can't see any development opportunities, you're unfairly treated, or you really don't think the job is for you – then you need to try and move on. That isn't always easy, but you might find the extra experience from your job helps. See p. 145 for ideas on moving on.

Anyway, this book suggests ways of putting more into and getting more out of your job. No job is perfect, but you can make most jobs work for you.

Getting to know your organization

Every organization has its own personality and characteristics – just like people. The places where you work may be friendly, aggressive, hectic, unhappy or sleepy. It won't take long to find out what kind of organization you're working for and decide whether:

● you fit in, it suits you down to the ground!
● it isn't really 'you', but you're happy to adapt while you're at work – because you enjoy your job and you're learning new things
● you don't fit in, and you don't think you'll ever really feel part of the organization.

All three reactions are fine. Everyone fits better into some organizations than others – just as everyone has different preferences for the type of friends they hang out with.

But don't make instant judgements when you're still new. Don't confuse feeling strange with feeling unhappy.

The trick to working out which of the three categories you fit into is to understand the organization's culture – the way it does things and why – and to work out the rules and customs that apply – just as if you were going to a foreign country you hadn't visited before.

Background

Find out what makes the organization 'tick' and what shapes its 'culture'. When was it set up? Has it changed size a lot over the years? Have there been any major recent changes (new location, buying another organization, selling part of its organization, joining together with another organization, changing its name, making lots of people redundant or taking on lots of new people)?

Have there been many changes at the top (chief executives, managing directors) or only a few? Who are the people with real influence (whatever their job title) and which groups of people make most of the key decisions?

What's its main aim – what does it say it's there to do (be the best at something, be a world leader in something, change something)? Does it have a 'vision' or a 'mission' statement (saying what it aims to do)? Does it have a list of principles or goals? Is it a local, national or international organization?

Finding out these things will help you to work out what kind of organization you've joined, and give you an idea about what kind of people work there! The next thing you need to find out is how it's structured.

Structure

Most organizations used to be organized like a pyramid, with one person in charge at the top and lots of people working at the bottom level (see diagram overleaf).

Due mainly to cost-cutting and technology, many organizations have reorganized or cut back on jobs, often shedding middle management. So many organizations now have 'flatter' structures

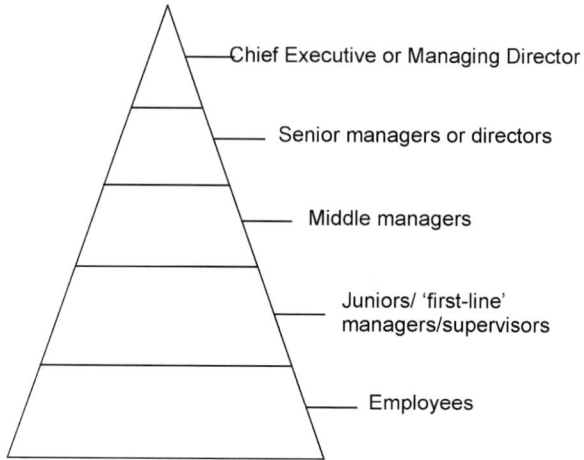

Chief Executive or Managing Director

Senior managers or directors

Middle managers

Juniors/ 'first-line' managers/supervisors

Employees

(with fewer layers than in the diagram above), or have even split into small units which manage themselves without layers of management. And, of course, small businesses can have very few managers (maybe only one or two). An organization's shape and structure usually affects its approach to work.

Approach

Some organizations are quite formal, expecting everyone to follow the rulebook. Others are more flexible (and often more friendly) wishing people to feel 'empowered' to get their job done in the best way possible, within reason. Most organizations are somewhere between the two – they have certain procedures (for dealing with money, communicating, getting decisions agreed, etc.) but they also try to get individual employees to take responsibility for their day-to-day work and give them some freedom in how they do their jobs.

You can often tell a lot about an organization from the way colleagues talk to each other (using first names or not), the way you have to dress at work, whether there are lots of small rooms, or big, open working spaces, whether senior people get out and about and talk to everyone else ('walking the job'), and whether people feel they work 'for' someone or 'with' a team. But whether you like it or not, you have to play by the rules of an organization in what you wear and how you behave.

Clothes

Most organizations have a 'dress code' – sometimes written down, but generally understood by people who work there. Some employees may have to wear protective or hygienic clothing, or a uniform, while others are expected to wear a suit, or can wear scruffy clothes (if they're working in a dirty environment, for example). It often depends on contact with customers and clients. In some organizations, there are different standards in different areas depending on people's jobs (some people wear suits, some wear jeans, for example) but in others, everyone wears roughly the same clothes. If you're not clear about what's appropriate and what's not, check with your manager.

There are a few other general standards of behaviour at work.

Common courtesy

This often involves behaviour in shared areas, like the photocopier room, kitchen, or drinks-making arrangements. 'Do as you would be done by' is a good rule. Everyone suffers when dirty cups are left in the sink or the photocopier's left without fresh supplies of paper.

When you are new to an organization make it your job to find out how things work. Are you expected to make or fetch a round of coffees, or does everyone get their own? And if there's a rota, make sure you take your turn. Don't use people's tools, equipment, desk or chair without asking and don't read other people's files or paperwork. Don't borrow things without asking.

Be considerate with colleagues. Don't get into the habit of asking for favours, however friendly you are and however nicely you ask. And treat everyone the same – don't have a pecking order. Be polite and pleasant to everyone, no matter what their job is.

Never shout or swear in the workplace (even if other people do it). Not only will you offend some people, but it doesn't give a good impression to customers and colleagues who may hear you.

Visitors, customers and clients

Here are some guidelines:

● Always put customers first and don't keep them hanging around.

- Never keep a visitor waiting, but if you have to, apologize in person and offer them refreshments and the use of the phone.
- When you greet people, call them by their name and tell them your own name. It's usually good to shake hands (while standing up).
- Put them at their ease with some pleasant comments, and don't forget to smile.
- If there are several people or a group, talk to them all rather than just to the closest. (If your conversation goes through an interpreter, direct your words to the visitor, not the person who is translating.)
- Allow visitors into and out of the lift first.
- If they are carrying more than one bag, offer to help.
- Offer to take their coat and tell them where the toilet facilities are.

You will be able to understand your organization by finding out a bit of background information, learning from what you see and hear, and being polite and friendly.

Point to remember
Every organization is different (and there may be a different culture and rules in different parts of the organization). Each colleague and customer is different. Find out about your organization, so you can do your job as effectively as possible.

Different people, different views and values

We live and work with a wide range of people – different ages, different backgrounds, different races, different sexuality, people with disabilities and so on. No two people are the same, we all have different skills, abilities and experience. And we all have different mixtures of attitudes and beliefs, which come from our values and affect how we behave (see diagram opposite).

Some organizations make the mistake of expecting everyone to behave in a similar way at work. That's not on for two reasons:

- everyone's different!
- its good to have teams with a mixture of people – so you can get different views and contributions.

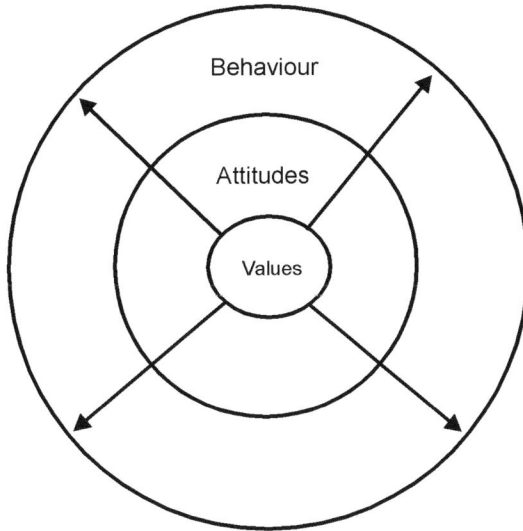

Worse, other organizations employ people who fit in with what makes them feel comfortable or what they think customers want to see. For example, they may prefer their managers to be white older men – and they would never think of employing someone in a wheelchair. This is not acceptable because:

● in the UK there are laws against discrimination based on sex, race and disability and there is a code of practice on age discrimination
● customers increasingly want to deal with organizations which have people like themselves working for them – on the basis that *'if there's nobody like me working there, how can they possibly understand what I really want?'*.

Organizations can have as many policies and practices as they like and still not provide fair and equal opportunities for employees and customers. That's because they are just telling employees to behave differently, but they're not getting to grips with people's attitudes and values.

People need a reason for changing their behaviour. Different reasons work for different people, but it's important to understand people's attitudes and beliefs (which come from their values) before trying to get them to change their behaviour.

Values, attitudes and behaviour

Values are what you pick up mainly early in life – from the people you grow up with, the places you see and the experiences you have. So if things were difficult when you were a child and you were always told 'you've got to be tough to survive', one of your values will be to be tough. Your attitude will be that people who show their feelings are weak. So you won't have much time for people who show their feelings and you will behave in an unsympathetic way towards them.

If, on the other hand, one of the values you pick up is about always sticking together as a family, your attitude will be that family comes before everything else and your behaviour will be to put your family first in terms of money, leisure time, emergencies, etc. So you may not be supportive towards people who put their job first, ahead of their family.

How someone behaves towards you at work is often not to do with you but more to do with them. And you will often react towards people based on how they measure up against your values and attitudes rather than what they're actually like and what they do.

We all need to make sense of the world in which we live and work in order to survive – and often have to do this based on first impressions not details of what's really going on. For example, a person might have been brought up in a family where all the men worked and the women stayed at home to look after the house and children. So their value might be *'men should work, women shouldn't'*. Their attitude towards working women is likely to be *'what the hell do you think you're doing here?'* or *'you've taken a man's job'* or *'you can't possibly understand the job, why are you bothering your pretty little head about it?'*. So their behaviour towards women colleagues could be to ignore them, not to take their contribution seriously, to criticize their work all the time, to get aggressive (as if that might make them give up work), or to keep referring to children. They can't see past their own values and attitudes and understand that people aren't good at their jobs just because they're a man – it's about having the right skills and experience.

Here's another example. Someone might have been brought up to believe that older people are out of touch and that young people cope better with busy lives. So their value is *'older people are past it'*. Their attitude towards older people will be lack of respect, boredom with their views, lack of patience *('you're so slow')*, not listening or learning. Their behaviour may be along the lines of *'I haven't got time to listen to you going on all the time'*, *'we need creative young people here, not people like you who are past it'* or *'if you can't cope with technology, you're no good to us'* (as if older people automatically can't use new technologies). Again, they're not looking beyond their own values and attitudes to see that older people are as varied as young people and they often bring more years of experience and a wider range of skills.

Going beyond first impressions

So you need to look beyond how people look to see what they can actually do. Don't make assumptions based on first impressions, including:

- their sex
- their racial, ethnic or cultural background
- their age
- any disability they may have
- their accent
- where they live
- whether they're married, single or living with someone
- whether they have children
- how they dress
- their hair
- their jewellery
- their qualifications and educational record
- whether they were convicted of any crime in the past, for which they have paid the relevant penalty.

One or two factors do not tell you about what a person can do. Just because they have things in common with someone you know or someone with whom you've worked before doesn't mean to say they'll be the same – as good or as useless! Just because your last colleague was a really effective woman in her early 30s doesn't mean another woman in her early 30s will be the same! Just because your last boss was a bullying man in his 50s doesn't mean you should steer clear of male bosses in their 50s! Treat everyone with respect and as an individual – they have values and attitudes which affect their behaviour at work (and outside work) and so do you. The trick is to make an effort to work well with all sorts of people.

As well as keeping an open mind about every different kind of person you deal with at and through work, you need to be confident about getting your message across in a way that works – for you and for those you're working with. Remember that an important part of successful communication is putting your message across so that it means something to the person you're communicating with. People from different backgrounds and cultures can react in different ways to the same message. For example, some cultures don't encourage regular eye contact, while others use it as a way of showing you're being honest and straightforward. You just have to accept and learn about these kinds of differences.

In some cases you might need to find different ways of working with people for practical reasons – for example, if they have a disability. Remember that people with disabilities are *people* first. Their disability (affecting their sight, hearing, mobility or health) is simply part of who they are and their way of life. Disabled colleagues don't want you to feel sorry for them or scared of them – they just want to get on with their work! And don't panic if you have to deal with disabled visitors or customers – they will let you know if they need any advice or help.

Everyone's different and in some cases you may stand out because of your sex, race, disability, age, accent, haircut… or any other factor. But you should be judged on what you can *do* not what you *look like* or *sound like* – and you need to treat others in the same way.

Working with different types of people

Occasionally someone will have a view about you (and people like you) which they won't change. No matter what you do, they won't take you seriously – or worse, they will tease you, bully you or even hurt you. In situations like this you need to decide whether their prejudice is worth trying to deal with. If you can accept it as just their view, that they don't know better, and if it isn't bothering you or preventing you from working well and safely – then you might decide just to get on and ignore it. But if it's upsetting, frightening or dangerous you *must* get things sorted out. Always try to tackle the problem not the person (see p. 137 on how to deal with various problems). If someone at work has a problem with who you are, the way you look, or where you come from, then don't get involved, get some advice. Your manager, personnel person or employee representative should be able to help. And if they can't help you, get advice from one of the organizations listed at the back of this book.

On the other hand, if you find yourself behaving badly towards certain types of people at work (for example, women, black or Asian colleagues, people with disabilities) then remember – *you've* got a problem that *you* need to deal with. Go back to p. 10 and think about the values that you grew up with and what they make you think about particular kinds of people. Now take a deep breath and think about the person you feel you've got a problem with. Are they really 'irritating', 'stupid', 'difficult' – or are they just different from you? Do you really have a problem with that person, or do they just remind you of someone you used to dislike or fear? The important thing is that they're trying to do the job they're paid for as well as they can. And you should be getting on with your job too – not spending time making rude comments, playing practical jokes or sending embarrassing e-mails. All those things can get you into trouble at work, and so can unkind or dangerous behaviour towards colleagues and customers.

So this isn't about having to like *everyone* you deal with or work with. It's about:

● giving everyone a fair chance before making any decisions about them
● not letting your instincts get the better of you – treat everyone with a bit of respect – just how you'd like to be treated
● not judging people on the basis of what you think about their 'type'
● remembering that everyone has a different mix of values which shape their attitudes and the way they behave

● not teasing or bullying people – it's not only unfair but your organization shouldn't let it happen (and it may also be illegal).

Point to remember

It's important to see people's differences as an advantage. Life would be very boring if we were all the same. You can learn things from watching how different people work, and teams need different types of people in them to be creative and effective.

Part Two

Skills

Skills

Everyone needs a mixture of different skills at work. Some skills are specific to certain jobs and need regular updating to cope with changes in the workplace and sector. Those who work in the information technology field, for example, have to keep up with almost daily changes and developments – and anyone who uses technology in their job needs to learn new things regularly to help them get the best out of, for example, their PC (personal computer), WP (word processor), laptop computer or, these days, even their high-tech phone. Many organizations arrange training for employees on skills which they need for key parts of their jobs. It's clearly in the organization's interest to make sure that everyone's doing their job as effectively as possible. But relatively few organizations offer training to all employees on some of the essential skills we all need at work, including how to:

● communicate effectively
● manage your time and workload
● use meetings effectively.

While it's worth trying to get some training on these things – and to develop and learn new skills in any areas you think are relevant – this part of the book sets out some basic ideas on how to get to grips with the essential skills for work.

Communication skills

Organizations increasingly succeed or fail on how they communicate – among employees, with each other, with customers, with suppliers, with competitors, with investors and shareholders. Saying what you mean – clearly and positively – and meaning what you say are vital skills for work and life. But effective communication is one of the hardest things to get right, all day and every day. So let's take a look at verbal communication, written communication and body language.

Verbal communication

These are the main things that stop you communicating effectively when talking to people:

- you're not clear about the message you want to give
- you're nervous and can't concentrate on what you're trying to say
- you're not aware of body language
- you waffle, use jargon or repeat yourself
- you put people off by using negative words and expressions
- the other person may not be listening, or they may hear what they want to hear rather than what you're actually saying.

Remember, you're only an effective communicator if you get your point across and make yourself understood. We regularly use expressions which put people off, irritate them or close a conversation down – phrases like:

'As you already know'
'I hear what you're saying, but ...'
'I know where you're coming from'
'It's not my fault'
'Do you understand what I'm telling you?'
'Calm down'
'You have to expect these types of problems'
'Well, most of our other customers realize'
'Of course, if it's a problem'
'You don't have to do business here, you know.'

Go on, be honest! How many of these have you used recently? The main things to avoid if you want to be a successful communicator are waffle, hype, jargon and clichés:

Waffle – meaningless 'padding' words and expressions, such as:

- er
- um
- you know?
- yeah?
- well
- sort of
- like
- kind of
- actually
- basically

Hype – words that over-emphasize a situation or feeling, such as:

- terribly
- brilliant
- enormously
- wonderful
- gorgeous
- incredible
- unbelievable
- outstanding
- horrifying
- tragic
- really
- honestly

Jargon – words, phrases or shorthand expressions which are used instead of existing expressions, such as:

Jargon	Meaning
A.S.A.P	as soon as possible
anon	soon (or abbreviation of anonymous/ not named)
diarize	to put in a diary
down time	free time/time off
empowerment	letting somebody do something
rightsizing or downsizing	reduce (by size or number of people)
surfing the net	using the Internet

- team player   someone who works well in a group
- window of   space or time to do something
  opportunity
- whistleblowing   telling the truth about something in
  your organization to the outside world

Clichés – overused expressions or catchphrases, such as:

Clichés	Meaning
at the end of the day	after all
do you have a window?	when are you free?
fully conversant with	understand
I request that you	would you...?
in this day and age	now
it is incumbent upon everyone	everyone should....
let's do lunch	shall we have lunch?
my people will speak to your people	we'll get in touch
to ensure beyond doubt	to make sure

There are also words, phrases or abbreviations used within a group of people (such as a department or team) which are meaningless to everyone else. Every organization has jargon shorthand, which is OK for internal use so long as everyone is familiar with the terms, but it should never be used to exclude colleagues from conversations or make it difficult for them to understand, nor should it ever be used when communicating with customers and suppliers. Strange abbreviations might look like:

MAT   Major Account Team (don't talk about MATs!)
CAT   Customer Adviser Team (don't talk about CATs!)
IHS   In-house services

So waffle, hype, jargon and clichés should be avoided in all communication. But what *should* you do? Generally, you should remember the ABC rule – appropriate, brief and clear, i.e.:

- appropriate – use the right words and tone for each situation

- brief – get to the point and don't repeat yourself (although summarizing is helpful)
- clear – say what you mean and mean what you say!

Face to face
This is perhaps the most powerful form of communication, if handled effectively. Think of all the face to face conversations and chats you've been involved in every day at work – and then stop and think about the impression you give through *what you say* and *how you sound*. Here are the things to look out for:

Words
Use appropriate words and phrases, always choosing the safe route if you're not sure. For example:

- first names are commonly used throughout the business world, but if it's not appropriate or you're not sure use Mr, Ms or Miss or a relevant title (Dr, Sir, Professor)
- don't use abbreviated names (like Bob instead of Robert or Naj instead of Najneen) unless you know it's appropriate. Avoid nicknames unless it's how someone chooses to be known. Never use secret nicknames for people as a joke among colleagues – they will slip out one day and may cause embarrassment and upset. *Never use terms with a sexist, racist or other offensive meaning* such as 'babe', 'love', 'darling', 'lads', 'darkies', 'queers', etc.
- Use straightforward language and expressions, and get straight to the point. It's good to start a conversation with a pleasant comment (*'how are you?' 'great news about the.......!' 'how was your journey?'* etc.) but then be focused and businesslike.

Tone of voice
If you sound bored or uninterested, your message will come across as boring and uninteresting! If you whisper, mumble or shout, you'll sound shy, unconvinced or bolshy. Try saying something like *'OK, I'll do it tomorrow then'* in the following different ways, and see how much difference your tone of voice makes to a message:

- sincere and friendly
- sarcastic

- angry
- upset
- patronizing.

Say what you mean and mean what you say
Don't play word games when communicating face to face. Be clear, get to the point and stick to it. If you don't know something, or can't agree to something, don't pretend or guess. It will only cause trouble later. Sensible, professional people prefer honesty. Colleagues prefer reliability. Everyone likes dealing with others who get to the point, explain things clearly and keep their promises.

Expression
The look on your face is vital in face to face communication. It's essential to make eye contact (even if the person you're talking to scares you for some reason – it's much better to look them straight in the eye – honestly), look interested (even when you're not), keep your mind on the issue you're discussing (don't think about going to the swimming pool later – you'll regret it when you miss hearing something important), and smile when appropriate (if they make a joke or a funny reference, when you agree on something, or to encourage them if they are looking anxious). Don't keep interrupting or butting in with your own comments or thoughts. Let the person to whom you're talking finish their sentences and pause before you start talking.

Try to keep the conversation moving on – don't keep covering the same old ground, otherwise nobody will ever get anywhere.

Asking questions
There are two main types of question, 'closed' and 'open'.
Closed questions narrow down the options for answering. For example:

- 'Is this your first job?'
- 'How many projects have you managed?'
- 'Is administration where you want to develop your career?'
- 'Do you feel confident about this training course?'

'Open' questions give options for answers and encourage people to give information. For example:

- 'Tell me more about the project'
- 'What kinds of things did you do as an administrator?'
- 'Can you explain a bit about your first job?'
- 'What sort of skills and experience have you got?'

Closed questions are OK if you just need a straightforward answer, but make sure your tone of voice doesn't make your question seem rude. Open questions are better for opening up the conversation and encouraging people to talk. If you are interviewing someone (for a project or for a job) you should use mostly open questions.

Networking
Be clear about what kind of networking you do at work and when you do it. For example, it's important to spend time chatting to a few colleagues on a personal level, to build up a social network within the workplace. You may or may not also see these people socially outside work, but you regard them anyway as people you get on well with. Everyone needs friends at work. This kind of networking should usually be done in your own time – during a coffee break, over lunch, on the way to the bus stop. Don't spend time chatting and joking instead of working!

There's also professional networking – where you build up extra trust and a good working relationship with an internal or external contact. Positive links with some colleagues and contacts provide good sources of help, advice and support within the workplace, as well as two-way links between different teams, departments and other organizations. But don't confuse your message by trying to talk about a serious issue in the bar, or being too jokey in a work meeting.

Body language
It's not just *what* you say, but also *how* you say it. We all give signals through gestures, facial expressions, how we sit and how we move. Don't forget that people from different backgrounds and cultures use gestures and facial expressions in different ways. For example, a lack of facial expression might not mean they're not listening. A calm response might not mean they're not excited by an idea. You just need to communicate as positively and openly as you

can – and watch their responses to check whether you're getting your message across in the right way. (See p. 37 for more details.)

Telephone

It will be a while before we all have 'videophones' in our workplace, so until then we've got to rely on the telephone for most of our distance communication. The same points apply as for face to face in terms of words and tone of voice, but some additional guidelines are:

● Don't pick up the phone to call someone without knowing what you want to say and why. It's not businesslike to chat away until you've remembered what you wanted to say, and it can be extremely irritating for the person you've called.

● Get comfortable with using answer machines and voice-mails. Always give your name, contact number and the time/date you called. Explain the reason for your call in two sentences at the most.

● Speak clearly, and smile when you're speaking if you want to make your voice sound positive to the person you're speaking to (no, really, it works!). And – for the same reason – sit up straight, don't slump forwards or backwards in your chair.

● When you answer the phone, wait until the handset is by your mouth (or the hands-free microphone is on) before you start talking. Always say 'hello' followed by your department (or organization, if it's a direct dial line) as callers sometimes miss the first few words (and it's better for them to miss 'hello' than your name). Answer the phone promptly (your organization may have guidelines on this).

● Learn how to make clear, brief notes when you're on the phone – it's amazing how many people can't read their own notes after they've put the phone down and their messages to colleagues are meaningless.

● If you call someone for a long discussion with them, always ask if it's a convenient time or if they'd prefer to talk later – and, if so, agree a time and who'll make the call.

● If you have organizational rules on answering the phone and taking messages, learn them and stick to them.

● Give clear signals when you feel the conversation is ready to end. Don't ramble on or let callers ramble on. You can best do this by summarizing briefly what's been discussed or agreed. *'OK, then. I'll get on with A and B, and I'll pass your number to Linford, who'll call you back by 4pm.'*

The following things are what irritate people most about phone conversations, so be warned!

● calls are not answered promptly, usually within three rings
● the call is answered and then held in a queue
● somebody picks up the phone but delays before answering
● muzack
● the call is diverted halfway round the building
● the caller is not given the option of being called back
● electronic answering with 'press button' commands
● 'while you wait' advertisements
● people who just say 'hello' when they pick up (not their name and department)
● people who sound bored, irritated or unhelpful
● not being asked if you would like to leave a message
● people who eat or smoke while on the phone
● people who are trying to hold two conversations at once
● salespeople who won't let you get a word in
● people who assume you're not busy and talk for ages
● sing-song voices when the phone is answered
● people who hang up without saying 'goodbye'
● people who waffle on without coming to the point
● people who say they'll ring you back and never do
● people who are aggressive over the phone because it's safe (they wouldn't dare say the same things face to face!).

Finally, avoid making personal calls from work. Most organizations accept that everyone needs to make the occasional call during work hours (to a bank or lawyer), but keep your chats with friends to a minimum or call them out of working hours.

Written communication
E-mails
E-mail (electronic mail) is a blessing and a curse. It's quick (almost instant, if someone's around to pick up their messages straight

away), saves paper (if people read off the screen rather than printing off messages) and, if necessary, people can respond immediately (using e-mail or another communication method). However, there's a danger of not thinking before you send e-mails (they look so harmless on the screen) and sending an over-enthusiastic or tetchy response. E-mails are not for chatting. They are an electronic form of sending and receiving messages, and they should be used when appropriate as a useful means of communicating at work. Think before you press that button!

Above all, avoid using e-mails to tease, embarrass – or worse – bully people at work. This is not only unprofessional (wasting time and abusing resources) but many organizations have policies which protect people from being harassed at work – and those who do it could be disciplined or dismissed.

Memos

This is a short way of saying 'memoranda' – 'memo' is short for 'memorandum'. Most organizations have a standard format for this type of written communication, which is a kind of internal letter, sent to one, several or many colleagues to pass on information. (Memos may occasionally be sent to people outside the organization, for example, to a group of consultants involved in a project, or to people who regularly work with the organization and understand its systems and language.)

The trick with a memo (as for all communication) is to:

- keep it short (one side of A4 paper at the most, if possible)
- make your points clearly
- use short paragraphs and bullet points
- use appropriate language and tone.

A good approach is to put yourself in the position of someone receiving your memo. You may know all the relevant background details, but do they? Is there any piece of helpful information you can include at the start? And remember, you want a positive response from your memo – colleagues responding within a certain deadline, or taking action, or giving you advice. So make sure you use the right tone – keep it as neutral as possible so you don't get people's backs up. Here's a checklist:

- who'll get the memo?
- what's their main priority or concern?
- what benefit will they get from reading the memo?
- is it clear what they need to do and by when?
- have you avoided critical or blaming phrases (don't say *'you failed to reply'* but say *'I haven't received a reply'* – don't say *'you don't understand . . .'* but say *'there seems to be a misunderstanding....'*).

Letters
Most organizations send frightening amounts of external mail – to customers, suppliers and contacts – and most of it will be letters. Sometimes they're mass produced ('mail merged', that is, the same letter but with addresses added from a mailing list) for marketing or publicity reasons. Mostly, though, they're individually produced letters, usually on the organization's stationery – and they're written by people who have different letter-writing styles and approaches.

You need to develop your own letter-writing skills – no matter how often or rarely you have to produce letters. Use the same overall communication rules, that this:

- keep it clear and to the point
- use short paragraphs and sentences
- use the language and tone appropriate for the person receiving the letter.

Things to avoid, as ever, are jargon, being pompous and using these kinds of over-the-top phrases (alternatives suggested):

Avoid	Use instead
request	ask
terminate	end
purchase	buy
please do not hesitate to	please
at this moment in time	now
endeavour to ascertain	try to find out

Plain English is increasingly seen as the way to communicate effectively. Fancy phrases and trendy words may sound good, but they don't get to the point and some people won't understand them.

Finally, always check spellings – words and people's names and addresses – and grammar (see p. 70).

Faxes

'Fax' is the short way of saying 'facsimile' which means copy. Fax machines are essential for sending a kind of photocopy over the telephone line. You should always use a title or cover sheet when you send any papers by fax machine (saying who the fax is for, who it's from and your contact details, the date of sending and the total number of pages being sent) – partly so those at the other end can sort out which bits of paper are for various people in their location, and partly because if you accidentally send it to the wrong place (by dialling the wrong number) the people who received it by mistake can get in touch with you. It's also worth phoning to check whether people have received your faxes, especially the important ones.

ISDN link

This is an increasingly popular way of sending documents quickly from one computer or word processor to another, by sending data down the phone lines. However, most people still use post, faxes, e-mail or the Internet.

Reports and summaries

You may have to write a report or summary, which means collecting and recording information for – perhaps – a project, or to help people make a decision. Don't panic! The usual communication rules apply, as ever (appropriate, brief, clear). And the good news is that most people don't read long reports or summaries, so it's better (and more effective) to concentrate on quality, not quantity.

It's important to give yourself enough quiet time to prepare, write and produce the report. You could use the following structure for a formal report – perhaps one for a customer or your organization's management team, but you could shorten or drop the sections marked ⋆ for a more informal report – a briefing document for colleagues, for example:

- title page
- contents/index
- summary/checklist of the whole report
- ⋆introduction

- findings
- conclusions
- recommendations for action
- *extra information (appendices)
- *acknowledgements for any help
- *references to any other reports used.

The most important part of any report is the summary or checklist at the front – especially as it's the only bit that most people have time to read! So put your efforts into making sure your summary contains:

- key points (including why the report has been produced)
- key findings (don't go into detail, just give the headlines)
- key conclusions and recommendations (there should be an obvious link between what you've found and what you suggest).

As ever, don't use jargon, avoid long-winded sentences, explain any technical terms you have to use, keep your sentences and paragraphs short, clear and to the point – and, above all, make sure the tone and style help get your point across.

Compliment slips

These are small pieces of paper, usually one third the horizontal size of a sheet of A4, blank except for the organization's name and contact details. They're usually sent to people outside the organization, paperclipped to things like a report or a brochure. You can print or handwrite (neatly) brief notes on compliment slips. You should usually at least put your name on the compliment slip, in case someone wants to get back in touch.

Other forms of communication

Making presentations

This sounds scary, but don't panic! The usual communication rules apply:

- be clear and avoid jargon
- keep it short and stick to the point
- get the tone right.

As with reports, give yourself time to think about what you want to say. You need to plan and prepare:

● your key points
● how you're going to explain or illustrate your points
● your notes
● any visual aids (flipcharts, overhead projector slides, computer generated slides).

It's difficult to brainstorm with yourself but you can use a 'think plan' (sometimes called a 'pattern note' – see below) to get your ideas going, like this:

● Take a plain sheet of paper and write the main theme in the centre.
● Write down all the ideas and thoughts you have on the subject, starting from the circle and branching out along lines of connecting ideas.
● Let your mind be as free as possible. Don't slow down by trying to sort out where each point should go in a list. Your ideas should flow easily.
● When you've finished, sort out all the useful ideas and work out an order for your presentation.

It's often worth getting someone else to look at your 'think plan' in case they can add something you may have missed.

Successful presentations

Preparation

- Use a 'think plan' to sort out what you want to say.
- Be clear about your aim.
- Decide what results you want and focus on them.
- Order your points so they make sense to your audience.
- Use simple, clear language, avoiding jargon.
- Aim your presentation at the people listening, using different ideas to get the attention of different groups.
- Think about possible questions beforehand, and try and answer them in your presentation.
- Prepare flip charts or overhead slides in advance. Handwriting on flipcharts is acceptable, but don't use handwritten overheads. (If you can't have overhead slides produced properly, it's better not to use them at all.)
- When using the flipchart use different colours. A flipchart written all in one colour is not clear or interesting.
- Avoid reading a script. Work out your full presentation and then put key words on cards to remind yourself of each point. Remember to number your cards and fasten them together in order!

Giving the presentation

- Always stand up – this helps people focus and hear more clearly.
- Don't fiddle with anything (earrings, pens, money in pockets, etc.) while you're talking.
- Look at your audience as you are talking to them. If you don't maintain eye contact with people, they will soon lose interest – and that makes a presentation even harder to do.
- Speak slowly and clearly and emphasize key words with a change of tone of voice. It's fine to pause (and you do need to breathe occasionally!).
- Remember that your audience probably want to hear what you've got to say.
- Make it clear at the beginning whether people can interrupt with questions – or whether they should make a note of them and save them to the end.
- Thank people at the end for listening.

Point to remember

Keep your communication appropriate, brief and clear – and use the best method of getting your message over. Always check to make sure you've got your point across – and if you haven't, try again!

Interpersonal skills

It's not just *what* you say at work that counts, but the *way* you say it – the way you behave and your body language. You'll know from experience that people often say one thing but mean something different! For example, if you turn up with a new outfit or haircut, someone may say '*it looks great*' but you can tell from the expression on their face and their tone of voice that they aren't really that keen.

Improving your interpersonal skills is about using the right kind of behaviour for each situation in order to make progress rather than causing problems. This doesn't mean you have to lie or be untrue to your feelings, but it does mean you have to be aware of the effect of your behaviour on other people and of their behaviour on you, so you can work together and communicate effectively.

Behaviour

There are four main types of behaviour linked to getting results. As we grow up we usually learn one of the following three:

Aggressive – people who behave aggressively usually get what they want (and there's trouble if they don't), but everyone else suffers and loses out.

Passive – people who behave passively usually end up doing what everyone else wants, so they lose out.

Manipulative – people who behave manipulatively get others to do what they want by making them feel guilty if they don't.

Which of these categories is most like you? (Be honest.) If you can't work it out, try checking these lists of characteristics:

Aggressive behaviour

What it looks like

- doesn't listen to others
- shouts or raises voice
- loses temper
- says 'I' not 'you' or 'we'
- refuses to back down or compromise.

Payoffs

- gets own way
- not argued with in future
- feels in control and in charge
- feels listened to and obeyed.

Problems

- people don't consult them or ask their advice
- 'obedience' to their request/command is short-term
- people feel defensive, resentful, frustrated
- people won't tell the truth because they're afraid of the reaction.

Passive behaviour

What it looks like

- doesn't listen to others
- doesn't say what he/she wants
- quiet, doesn't speak out, especially in public
- does things resentfully
- says 'you' rather than 'I' or 'we'
- complains and whines a lot
- always feels hard done by
- doesn't get own way.

Payoffs

- doesn't have to think or come up with solutions
- gets left alone.

Problems

- people don't consult them or ask for their views
- feel frustrated, guilty
- end up doing things they don't want to do or don't agree with.

Manipulative behaviour

What it looks like

- sulks
- sarcastic
- doesn't come straight to the point
- plays on people's feelings, particularly of guilt.

Payoffs

- gets own way
- feels in control.

Problems

- people feel confused, angry, guilty
- not believed or trusted
- people are reluctant to approach them or ask for their advice.

Of course, very few of us behave in the same way all the time. We tend to start off by being polite and positive when we communicate, but if things get difficult and we aren't getting what we want, we slip back into one of the three behaviours listed above, so we need to be assertive instead.

Assertiveness

Work often involves reaching a situation where everyone involved feels they've got an acceptable result — maybe not the ideal outcome, but at least a compromise. The best way to do this is for people to develop their *assertiveness* skills. It can be hard to learn and hard to stick to, but it does help every day, at work and outside work. It's worth the effort.

So what's assertiveness all about? Assertive behaviour (unlike being aggressive, passive or manipulative) is about:

- understanding what kind of person you are and why you behave as you do
- being clear about your priorities
- being aware that you have rights, but others do too
- accepting that you have responsibilities, just like everyone else
- changing your mind when appropriate
- being prepared to be flexible and find some common ground
- making choices
- behaving like a grown-up person (not like an aggressive, passive or manipulative child)
- accepting that you have to think before you speak and act.

Assertive behaviour isn't about getting your own way cleverly. Winning's great, but it's not good if one person or team gets their way all the time at work. One trendy phrase is *'getting to a win-win situation'*, which means trying to make sure that everyone involved feels they benefit from a decision in some way.

Getting people to agree on straightforward work issues is hard enough, but it's even more difficult if you have to deal with a problem or make a complaint. Under those circumstances, the assertive approach is to:

- Think before you do or say anything!
- Remind yourself that you want to make things better in the long run, not just make yourself feel better for a bit. For example, if a colleague has let you down (not meeting a deadline, sending you the wrong information, etc.) the first reaction is to want to have a go. It might make you feel better, but it won't prevent the same thing from happening again. And it's likely to make the person you're shouting at feel cross or upset.

- Put yourself in the other person's shoes – how would you feel? Think of the various ways in which they might react, and work out which approach is likely to get the most positive result.
- Be prepared to take a different approach, maybe at a different time or place.
- Follow the assertiveness guidelines below so you can feel confident about handling the situation even if gets difficult.

Getting information assertively

- explain what you want and why
- don't over-explain – keep it simple!
- ask 'open' questions
- don't interrupt while others are talking
- look encouraging – nod, smile and make notes as appropriate.

Giving information assertively

- say what you're explaining and why
- keep to the point – there's no need to keep repeating yourself
- summarize and make any suggestions for the way forward.

Disagreeing assertively

- explain where people agree and disagree
- use evidence, don't just keep talking about opinions
- focus on *what's* wrong not *who's* wrong
- be flexible and listen to other points of view
- find the common ground.

Asking assertively

- don't go round in circles – get to the point
- keep personalities out of it – focus on what's needed
- be clear and straightforward about what's needed and why
- be prepared to find another way forward if your request is refused.

Saying 'no' assertively

- explain why you can't agree – keep it short
- apologize and be polite – but don't go over the top

- keep personalities out of it – focus on what's being discussed
- if you're asked again, don't change you mind and give in – just repeat the '*sorry, no*' bit, and make sure you've made the reason clear.

Coping assertively with being angry or upset

- don't shout, don't cry, don't swear, don't use over-the-top language
- make it clear *how you feel*
- be specific about the problem (is it that they were late, or is it that they didn't call to say they'd be late)
- don't have a go at the person in general – talk about their *behaviour* on this occasion (avoid '*and another thing . . . . I've always hated you*')
- suggest how it could be different and better *('it would help me if, next time, you...')*
- don't over-emphasize or under-emphasize – (don't say '*I was a bit surprised*' when you mean '*I was very hurt*' or '*I was extremely angry*' when you mean '*I was irritated*').

Being assertive isn't about being nice, or being pushy. It isn't about speaking in a quiet controlled way or speaking in a loud clear voice. It's about **saying what you mean and meaning what you say** – openly and honestly – and about trying to get results that meet everyone's needs as far as possible. Use tone of voice, words and gestures to make your point. Check that you've got your message across. Explain or repeat if you're not making progress. Look at the situation from other people's point of view. Being assertive (rather than aggressive, passive or manipulative) will make you more effective at work.

Assertive body language

Sometimes you may think you've said one thing, but your body language gives off different signals. In fact, it's estimated that over half of the messages people get come through *how we look* not *what we say*. Here are some do's and don'ts.

Do	Don't
− stand up straight	− hunch up
− face people	− slouch
− look people squarely in the face	− look down or away
− stand firmly and squarely	− balance on one leg, fidget
− walk confidently	− creep around
− greet people openly	− smile shyly
− speak confidently	− mumble
− use gestures positively	− fiddle with your hands
− move closer to the other person	− wander around
− lean forward slightly in your chair	− lean back in your chair with both hands behind your head
− avoid sudden movements	− move forward suddenly
− look at the other person's face	− stare at the other person
− smile when pleased	− have an '*I've heard it all before*' smile
− nod your head occasionally as the other person is talking	− raise your eyebrows in surprise or amazement
− keep arms uncrossed	− have your arms crossed

The way you look gives strong messages about what you're thinking and feeling. It's important to understand the vibes people get when they're with you − you may think you're saying one thing, but those around you are picking up something different. Just to test this, try saying the following things to a friend − the first time looking them in the eye and smiling, the second time looking away and frowning. See the difference?

- *Hello, how are you?*
- *Oh good − I wanted to have a word with you.*
- *I need to see you for ten minutes today.*
- *I didn't get the papers you said you were sending − is there a problem?*
- *Somebody told me you've had a change of plan − what do I need to know?*

It's helpful to use body language in positive ways – or at least to stop it being negative. It can help you feel better and more confident about yourself. For example, if you're anxious about something and it shows through your body language, you won't be able to convince people you're confident, no matter what you say. These are the kinds of things to look out for (watch for them in others and avoid them yourself!).

Looking nervous

- crossed arms and/or legs
- carrying books or papers across your chest
- sitting in a slumped position
- sitting on the edge of the chair
- clutching hands together
- tapping foot
- drumming fingers on table
- biting nails
- fiddling with jewellery or hair
- covering your mouth with your hand when you talk
- rocking in your chair
- scratching or itching
- clearing your throat too much
- straightening tie
- playing with watch or cufflinks
- hands in pockets.

Looking aggressive

- arms folded across chest
- staring or pointing
- making your hand into a fist
- standing or leaning too close to someone.

Being rude

- working while someone is talking to you
- puffing and sighing
- whispering so others can't hear you
- packing up papers and folders before a meeting has finished
- shaking hands too hard or not firmly enough

- yawning
- looking at your watch.

Fiddling

We all fiddle if we're nervous. It may not be the reason for doing the following things, but they will still make you look nervous. Often we don't know we've got the habit and are surprised when someone points it out. Find out what your pet fiddle is – maybe you do it more often when you get tense. See if any of these sound familiar:

- blinking a lot
- fiddling with rings, watches, earrings, chains
- pushing glasses higher up your nose
- playing with paper clips
- jingling money in pocket
- picking at fingernails
- twiddling bits of hair
- smoking.

Hand signals

Body talk says a lot, so it's worth checking that your hands are helping you communicate, not giving a wrong or infuriating message. Here are some of the hand movements to avoid:

Silly

- waving your hands, pens or spectacles around a lot
- banging the table when laughing (or instead of laughing) at a joke.

Irritating

- fiddling with jewellery
- 'air quotes' (indicating 'speech marks' by jiggling your fingers in the air, arms apart).

Rude

- cleaning ears or nails
- any gesture which means something rude or sexual.

Comfort zones

We all have four main comfort zones – the right kind of distance we need between ourselves and other people in order to feel comfortable. If people stand or sit closer than we expect them to, it can make us feel uncomfortable or frightened. Here are the zones:

Public: for strangers, or an audience if you're making a presentation

Social: for people we know, but not all that well

Friendly: for people we're with at a party or in the bar, or for close colleagues

Close: for immediate family members and lovers.

We all know how irritating or upsetting it can be if someone gets closer to us than feels right. These are the kinds of rules to follow in the workplace:

● don't invade someone else's desk, chair or work area – or the place where they keep their work things
● don't make friendly gestures (putting arms around shoulders, moving seat closer, patting on the back, arm or knee) unless you're clear that you're both in the same comfort zone (friendly)
● don't stand or walk too close to people
● avoid touching or brushing against people wherever possible
● don't hang around or try to be 'social' or 'friendly' unless you're sure that the other person's in the same mood
● if you have to get close to people (crowded offices, lifts, rest rooms, etc.) don't make eye contact, smile or lean towards someone – unless you bump into a close colleague or you end up standing next to someone you haven't seen for ages (in other words, it's a social or friendly situation).

The trick is to keep things balanced – stay in the same comfort zone as the people you're with – so no one feels threatened. The one 'touching' exception is shaking hands. Most people are happy to shake hands, especially when they first meet in a work context. It's a good way to acknowledge each other or introduce yourselves. Make sure to give a firm, brief handshake (your hand shouldn't feel like a limp fish or an iron glove), always look the person in the eye while you're shaking and smile pleasantly. And only use one hand – not two!

Bad body talk

Some people use tricks to make other people feel small – and to make themselves feel important. It's a kind of bullying, it happens in every workplace, and you need to know what it looks like so you can deal with it if it becomes a problem. Things to look out for include:

- standing behind someone's chair and reading over their shoulder while they work
- leaning over or sitting on someone's desk
- staying slumped in your chair when you greet someone
- giving an 'iron glove' handshake
- standing too close when you talk to someone
- smoking in someone else's space
- shouting orders
- swearing
- continuing to work when colleagues talk to you
- drumming the tips of your fingers together when listening to someone
- leaning back in your chair with your hands behind your head
- sitting with your feet on your desk
- staring
- touching or patting people when they aren't happy about it
- ignoring people when they greet you
- going into meetings with your pager or mobile phone switched on (except in a really urgent situation).

Don't let people who behave like this get you down. Even if they're making out that you've got a problem, they're really the ones with a problem. Here are some suggestions:

- Keep calm and think before you say or do anything.
- If someone stands too close, look them straight in the eye, take a step back, then glance at the gap between you and then look them in the eye again.

- If someone ignores you when you say '*hello*' or '*goodbye*' each day, then just carry on saying '*hi*' and '*bye*' – don't stop talking to them or get rude (don't sink to their level).
- If someone carries on working when you're trying to talk to them, then pause, smile pleasantly, wait for them to look up and say something like '*can I just explain this?*' or '*if this isn't a good time, when can I come back?*'. Don't get upset or cross.
- If someone reads your screen or paperwork over your shoulder, say pleasantly but firmly something like '*look, I know you don't mean to make me feel uncomfortable, but I find it difficult to work while you're standing there.*'
- If someone smokes or swears or shouts in your space, try something like '*I'm sorry, but please could you stop doing that here? Thanks.*'

For other tips see p. 35 for details about being assertive (firm but fair!).

Sitting and standing
It really looks better (and it's better for you) to sit and stand up straight. When you have to sit or stand for a long period of time, it's easy to slump and stoop, but not only will it make you look tired (and not give a very positive impression to those around you) it will also make you feel tired –and, over time, it will affect your fitness. Whether you've been sitting or standing, you can straighten out with a few simple stretching movements – but only do this in your breaks (not in your work area). Try:

- standing up straight, shoulders back, chin up, eyes forward
- breathing slowly and steadily – filling your lungs, holding your breath, breathing out slowly
- sitting on a chair, lifting your feet off the floor, rotating your feet at the ankles
- stretching out your arms level with your shoulders, moving them slowly backwards and forwards (making sure you don't hit anyone)
- walking around whenever you can (take the stairs instead of the lift, walk over to people's desks, don't phone them!)
- not crossing your legs (can give off bad vibes – making you look anxious or nervous – as well as being bad for your muscles and circulation)

● not crossing your arms (looks defensive and is bad for posture)
● not perching on the edge of your seat
● not leaning forward on your elbows
● not resting your chin on your hands.

Conversations

You can often pick up what someone is really thinking and feeling from what they do rather than say. Here's a checklist:

'I don't agree'

- eyes narrowing or closing
- glancing away
- leaning backwards
- shaking of the head
- frowning.

'You're beginning to irritate me'

- foot tapping
- fingers drumming on desk
- fiddling with pen
- sighing
- folding arms
- looking away or looking at watch.

'Help! I'm feeling nervous – back me up here'

- touching neck or ears
- touching or patting hair
- looking around nervously
- frowning
- biting nails
- chewing pen
- fiddling with jewellery, watch or tie.

'I'm much more important than you'

- sitting in a big, imposing chair
- tilting backwards in chair
- putting feet on desk
- pointing aggressively

- making aggressive eye contact
- being over-friendly (like putting an arm round someone's shoulders).

Point to remember
How you say things is as important as what you say, so use positive body language and develop an assertive approach.

Meetings

Sometimes it seems as though work for some people consists only of meetings. You call to speak to someone and they're 'in a meeting', you contact someone else to schedule something into their diary and you're told 'they can't make it that afternoon, they've got a meeting'.

Meetings between two or more people can be the most effective way of raising and discussing issues in order to decide on a way forward. A properly run one-hour meeting can save hours of telephone time, pages of memos and days of delay while ideas are passed between those involved. It's also most effective, wherever possible, to communicate face to face. And if there are any really tricky or sensitive issues, it's easier to sort them out behind a closed door, with all those involved, rather than on paper and over the phone. So, what types of meetings are there, how do you make best use of them, and if you're asked to set up and run a meeting, what do you do?

Successful meetings

A meeting should always have a clear objective if it's going to be successful. In order for you to make a useful contribution to the meeting – or to get something useful out of it – you need to know what it is for.

If you haven't been sent an agenda containing relevant details (time, place, those attending, objective, issues to be covered) then get hold of whoever set up the meeting and check. Not only will that prevent you from turning up at the wrong place or time (yes, it often happens – especially when different people get different telephone messages) but, more importantly, it enables you to *prepare*. Here's an example of what an agenda might look like.

Sales team meeting agenda

Date: 19 January 1999
Time: 0930 – 1100 hours
Venue: The Boardroom

Attendees: Sunita, Andrew, Lo (Chairing), Bradley

Time	Item	Contributor
0930	Welcome and apologies for absence	Chair
0935	Sales figures	Sunita, Bradley
0945	IT Project – update and report on progress	Andrew
1005	How the new IT system will improve sales – discussion	All
1030	Communication – how to communicate the new system to the rest of the organization	All
1045	Any other business	Chair
1100	End of meeting	

Preparation will often just be some thinking to get your ideas clear on the issues to be discussed. Sometimes it may involve checking a few facts or pulling together some relevant paperwork. Occasionally you may be asked to talk about a particular agenda item – another good reason for always checking agendas in advance. It's amazing how many people setting up meetings will 'volunteer' others to make a contribution just by assuming they'll be happy to do so. And if you are likely to be making a specific contribution, don't just think about what you're going to say, but also what other people's responses might be – and how you might respond to their comments.

Remember – meetings are *not* for general conversation and chat but for structured discussion, focused on specific issues, usually within a fairly tight timescale. There should always be someone 'in the chair' to keep an eye on the time and steer the meeting. Here are some suggestions on tactics for good meetings:

- Always arrive early (around five minutes is ideal).
- Remember to take the agenda, any relevant notes from previous meetings and any papers you've prepared.
- Take paper or a notebook and a pen.
- If you want to make a comment, jot down a note of the key point(s) you want to make. It's helpful to have something to refer to if you're side-tracked or interrupted when you're speaking.
- If you make any comments, keep them short and clear.
- Be positive and listen to everyone else's points – meetings are good opportunities for learning things. Never get aggressive or argumentative.
- Don't be afraid to ask questions. You can't continue to make an effective contribution to the meeting if you're not clear about all the areas covered – besides which, if you're not clear, it's likely that others won't be either!
- If you're asked to follow something up after the meeting, make yourself a clear *action note* and check on the deadline. Your action note might look like this:

Action:
Check the budget figures – do a chart and send to xyz to arrive by Friday. Contact team managers by following Tuesday.

- If you're asked to do something as a result of the meeting and you know you can't, then explain the problem and sort out an alternative (perhaps someone will take some action instead, or they'll work with you).
- Always do what you say you'll do following a meeting. It's not only what you're paid for (doing your job) but it's good

to be seen as reliable. However, if things crop up and you really can't take action as agreed, then contact the person who chaired the meeting, explain the situation and get their advice.

Setting up a meeting

What if you need to set up a meeting yourself? Well, all the same rules apply, except you're the one making the arrangements. Here's a simple checklist.

Objective – be clear about the meeting's objective.

Participants – decide who needs to be there to make the meeting effective.

Items to cover – list the different issues relating to the objective and put them in the most logical order for discussion.

Timescale – first, check on how soon you need to have the meeting (does it have to happen before any other planned activities, for example) and second, decide roughly how long it will take to cover everything. (Remember that people can't concentrate and work effectively for more than about an hour – especially in the really focused way expected in meetings – so if the meeting has to be longer than an hour, schedule in short breaks. Ten minutes is usually enough for a break.)

Practicalities – check whether you'll need to book refreshments or lunch, as well as a flipchart or overhead projector. Also, choose the best room layout for the type of meeting. Options include:

– 'square or circle' – chairs and (usually) tables in a square or circle
– 'horseshoe' – three sides of a rectangle
– 'cabaret' – several small circles or squares around the room
– 'boardroom' – long rectangle
– 'theatre' – seats in rows facing forwards, for a big meeting with presentations.

Venue – you may decide this before you start contacting people, or you may contact people first and ask them where would be most convenient.

Agenda – sometimes you'll have to get everyone you need – otherwise there's no point in running the meeting. On other occasions, it's an 'attend if you can' situation – you send out the agenda to everyone who's invited and ask people to let you know if they can't be there – in which case they're usually listed as having sent their 'apologies'. Sending out the agenda in advance (making sure it gives everyone enough time to prepare) usually acts as confirmation that the meeting's going ahead, where and when.

Chairing – to be effective, meetings need someone to steer discussion, keep an eye on the time or, occasionally, sort out any arguments or confusion. The person 'in the chair' should start on time, welcome everyone and thank them for attending, list any apologies from people who can't be there, explain the purpose of the meeting, get discussion going on each item (introducing anyone who's listed as making a contribution to those items), make sure that the meeting runs to time, check that everyone's clear about actions (including who's said they'll take them) and confirm whether notes of the meeting will be sent round. It's best if the chair manages everyone else's contributions rather than getting too involved themselves.

Minutes – notes taken during meetings are often called 'minutes'. The most useful meeting notes are short, clear and action-focused (more who's *doing* what rather than who *said* what). They should be sent immediately after the meeting.

Types of meetings
All meetings should have a focus, but some have a particular purpose, such as:

Brainstorming meetings – this isn't the polite word for chaos! It's about generating lots of ideas and creative thinking, and it can be helpful as the first stage in solving problems. Here are the rules:

● keep it short – 30 minutes is probably the maximum time for effective brainstorming
● keep the group small – 6 to 12 is ideal
● involve a good mix of people, but remember that certain people (senior managers, perhaps) might stop others from being as free-thinking and creative as they could be
● keep it informal – a circle of chairs with no table and just a flipchart works well

- the person in the chair needs to stop people talking over each other and to make sure everyone has a say
- the person writing the ideas on the flipchart needs to write everything down (not change or edit things as they see fit)
- there shouldn't be any discussion of ideas – brainstorming's about having ideas not deciding between them
- sift them later into good ideas for immediate use, interesting ideas to be thought about or passed on, and ideas which weren't appropriate (maybe tried before) or just silly.

Problem solving meetings – this kind of meeting aims to tackle one particular problem. The meeting should:

- identify the problem – write it down in one straightforward sentence so that everyone is clear
- think about the various aspects – what are the hard facts, what are people's views and feelings?
- decide on the next step – finding a solution or tackling one aspect?
- look for ways forward – what would solutions look like, are there alternatives, what seems the best option?
- decide on action and next steps.

Team meetings – this doesn't necessarily mean the whole department, or the people you work regularly with – it could also be a project team (people from different teams across the organization). Whatever 'team' it is, there's a danger that people will get bored with any meeting – particularly those held regularly – which seems to be just a 'get-together' rather than for a real reason. So, team meetings need to be:

- as short as possible
- focused on a clear objective, with an agenda sent round in advance
- participative – if it's a team, everyone should feel able to contribute (with no blame or shame about getting things wrong)
- successful – if team meetings aren't helping team members to work together more effectively, change or stop the meetings!

One to one (1:1) meetings – this kind of meeting:

- is a face to face discussion between you and your manager
- looks at the whole job – not just one or two bits of it
- is structured, not just a chat
- looks at past and current activities, plus future developments
- is recorded and dated, and a copy kept with previous 1:1 notes
- focuses on you, and allows a bit of time to look at how things are working between you and your manager
- ends up with action points and deadline dates
- finishes with agreement on the date for the next 1:1 meeting.

Other kinds of meetings are to:

- get to know people and exchange information or ideas
- sell something, or present a proposal
- discipline someone
- update someone
- manage or "appraise" someone
- hear a grievance or complaint.

In each case, the same rules about objectives, preparation, timescale and notes apply. It's worth mentioning three other aspects of meetings.

First, there's the 'can you meet and eat' dilemma. Many people have business meals and some people seem to be good at covering an agenda (written or unwritten) over food and drink. However, it's better – wherever possible – to keep meeting and eating separate, because:

- eating should be a sociable activity, for a break in a busy working day (see p. 124 on work/life balance)
- it's difficult to get the formal/informal balance right over food
- it's difficult to make notes.

Second, most people spend time in meetings with others who have different backgrounds, characters, and approaches. You need to be able to respond positively to different inputs. But there are also some specific cultural differences between the way people work together and communicate – and this affects meetings and their outcomes. With extensive European and global contact, it's important to feel comfortable with other cultures' approaches. So if your organization includes people from different countries, or if you are likely to work with people from different backgrounds, it's worth doing some research on their approaches and priorities (see p. 8 on diversity).

Third, with sophisticated technology, you may have 'tele-meetings' – where everyone is in a different place but linked by telephone (usually called a 'conference call') where everyone can hear what's going on, or by video (called 'video conferencing'). This can seem odd until you get the hang of it, but the main thing is – don't all try to talk at once. It can be expensive but can also save lots of travel and accommodation time.

Things to avoid in meetings

We all come across people at work (colleagues and customers) who use meetings for their own purposes rather than to help tackle the overall objective. Here are some of the characters to watch out for (and avoid copying):

The show-off – who wants to display as much of their knowledge as possible, regardless of the topic being discussed – or how much they know about it. Often loud and tactless, butting in with jokes or comments that disrupt the flow of conversation. May also use long words or jargon unnecessarily.

The schemer – with a very strong 'personal agenda' who has perfected the art of saving their contribution until the moment when it will have most impact – usually towards the end of the meeting – to prevent others reaching a decision that might be inconvenient for their personal plans. Often one of the organization's survivors because they've become good at protecting their own position by manipulating decisions in meetings.

The bully – who makes use of their position to push others around in meetings. Usually someone in a senior or powerful role who is scared of others with talent, and therefore likes to remind everyone how important they are by using various tactics: raising their voice, exclaiming loudly (*'I don't believe it!'*, *'If you could see yourselves'*, etc.), getting up and marching around, using threats (*'You're in for serious trouble if you don't sort this out in the next ten minutes'*).

The 'yes' person – who watches how things are going and then sides with whichever individual or group seems to be most influential. Often someone who puts more energy into looking good in the organization than into doing a good job.

The expert – who knows a lot about relevant issues but isn't good at communicating effectively, delivers mini-lectures which take ages to get to the point (by which time others have switched off and started to write their shopping lists). Often very bright but not able to make an effective contribution to meetings.

The presenter – who can't contribute to a meeting or make a point without drawing a diagram or listing some bullet points on a flipchart. Often a creative person, but their obsession with making mini-presentations puts others off.

The token gesturer – who will always say something at any meeting whether it's useful or not – just to justify being there. Often someone who switches off during meetings apart from one point at which they'll make some comment – usually repeating what someone else has said.

The nodder – who spends most of the time in meetings looking interested/concerned/wise/involved and nodding a lot, apparently in support of what others are saying. They very rarely make any original contribution.

The head downer – who doesn't want to commit themselves to any particular view or decision in public. They keep their head down to avoid confrontation and taking any decision.

The sleeper - yes! Some people doze off in meetings (and who can blame them sometimes?). It may not seem particularly helpful and it's not to be recommended, but they could really feel the need to sleep (if they've got young children or have been ill, for example).

Point to remember
Meetings are an effective use of time if they are properly planned and well run. Don't become a meetings bore, by always being in a meeting – and don't use meetings to cover your own agenda rather than the one set for the meeting.

Managing your time and workload

The world is divided into those who always meet or beat deadlines – and the rest of us. Time is like water – there's always far too little or, occasionally, far too much.

Managing your time and your workload is a vital skill. It's important for:

● **you**, so you can do your job to the best of your ability, you don't get stressed out through constant pressure and worry, and you give a positive message to others around you
● **your manager and colleagues**, who need you to play your part in the team
● **your organization**, which only functions if everyone does their bit in the right way, at the right time.

Time and workload management is mainly about organization and self-discipline. You know almost exactly how much time you've got for doing all the things you have to do (say seven hours a day, five days a week) or the amount of time during which you are required to work (say, an eight hour shift). The trick is to *plan* what you can achieve within that time and *manage* whatever else crops up.

How you use your time

If there's any choice about what to do first – or what to bother doing at all – it's really tempting to focus on what you enjoy and forget about the rest. This is a bad habit! The way to break this habit is to start with the things that are best done first or that you have to do first (because of other people's deadlines) and then work your way logically through everything else. Here's an idea on how to check what you're spending your time on, so that you can improve your time and workload management.

Time log

A daily time log is a simple record to show where you have spent your time (a bit like looking at your bank statement to see where you have overspent and where you have cut back). You need to find out whether you're staying within your time budget.

Analyzing your time log highlights certain key areas where you can begin to save time. Could you do all your photocopying or faxing at the same time? Do you need to put aside some time for writing reports each month, or time for dealing with correspondence? Are you organizing cleaning the machines in the most logical order? Can you save time by planning your phone calls or customer chasing more effectively?

Morning time log								
Minutes								
Start time	Finish time	Activity	1	2	3	4	5	6
			correspondence	meeting	break	action	phone	customer
0900	0910	Coffee			10			
0910	1040	Meeting		90				
1040	1115	Morning correspondence	15			15		
1115	1215	Replying to post	30			30		
1215	1240	Interruption						25
1240	1305	Sandwich			25			
1305	1315	Telephone call					10	
TOTALS			45	90	35	45	10	25

So by using your time log you can work out where you're using time effectively and where you might be wasting it. You will know how much time you have and what to spend it on. You can then begin to prioritize your time and work.

Consider the following questions:

● What is the main purpose of your job? What are you expected to achieve?
● What do you need to do to achieve that purpose? What are the specific things that you do across the whole of your job?

The answers to these questions give you your priorities. When deciding what you should tackle first, remind yourself of your main job purpose.

Managing priorities

There are two main categories for your work – **reactive** tasks and **proactive** tasks. Reactive tasks are what you do as routine, in response to something happening, or at someone's request. Proactive tasks are what you can plan in advance. It's helpful to work out roughly what percentage of your working day/week you spend on each type of task. Clearly it varies, but it's good to get a rough idea.

Whatever the percentages are for you, this is your real world. You need to live in it. That means being realistic about how you plan your time. Most people have a tendency to plan their days using up every minute of their time, and then they wonder why they have problems getting through everything. It's usually because they haven't taken into account the things that go wrong or take up more time than expected. You need to plan for things to go wrong. Always leave a bit of spare time if you can – not leave things until close to the deadline when they're due to be finished – and always plan well in advance.

Remember, computers break down, production lines go wrong, supplies are delivered late – so plan ahead and leave flexibility for emergencies.

Planning ahead

Don't just write down what you know you have to do (shifts, meetings, etc.) but also do a time planner for everything you need to do. Your time planner might look something like this:

Monday	1030: Meeting with Z	pm: paperwork
Tuesday	day off	
Wednesday	am: call A&B	1100 onwards: start drafting report
Thursday	0930: C, D & E visiting site	pm: training course
Friday	am: paperwork	pm: book service visits
Saturday	day off	
Sunday	all day – duty shift	
Next week's priorities: set up project team, finish report		

And don't forget that you'll always underestimate the time things take! There's plenty of emergency time in the planner above, and you need to keep it like that for any extra tasks that crop up as you go along.

Managing deadlines

There are three main tricks to managing deadlines.

First, build in extra, spare time as explained above.

Second, always be clear about deadlines – if someone suggests one and you can't meet it then say so! Use your assertiveness skills to find a deadline that you can both meet. And if they really can't change the deadline and you have to agree, then ask for help, move some of your other deadlines to make enough space (in which case, make sure you agree the new deadlines with everyone else who's relying on you).

Third, sort your tasks into three groups: urgent (do it immediately), important (schedule time to do it as soon as possible), and general (do it when you can – book in some time in a week or so). You need a system for keeping things in date order, so you pull out the right bits of information each day (this is usually called a 'bring forward' system, either kept in a file or on computer, and it should be checked and updated every day).

And don't forget – if you need people to help you, always give them a deadline for action. If it's a long way ahead (several weeks or months) it's usually worth sending a reminder note or phoning to chase them before the date.

Other time management tips
If you can do something straight away then do it. Don't keep putting things back in files, and don't keep putting things off – you're just wasting time. If you get a memo and you can deal with it immediately, then take some action, sort it out and move on. If a machine needs repairing or cleaning, plan in some time soon and get it done. If new supplies need ordering, get on the phone now, don't leave it (you'll forget, and then there will be a panic when things run out).

While these guidelines have focused mainly on work, the same things apply to the rest of your life. Nobody has enough time, so it's good if you can plan ahead for the things you do outside work (evenings, time off, weekends, holidays) in order to get the most out of your leisure time and keep your stress levels under control (see p. 134). Remember – the same rules apply:

● Always sort things out straight away if you can – don't leave them hanging over you (bills, phone calls).
● Always plan ahead so you can meet or even beat deadlines (booking holidays, cinema tickets, paying bills).
● Always build in a bit of spare time for *you* – you need it.

Point to remember
Time and workload management is an essential skill, enabling you to do your job and cope with things at short notice. A bit of time spent planning always pays off.

Managing projects

Projects are like stories – they should have a beginning (when someone decides that something needs to be done, set up or reviewed), a middle (when the work is done) and an end (the outcome, decision or report back).

The bad news is that projects are also like people. They can be unpredictable and difficult to manage! The good news is that there are ways of managing projects to get the results you need.

First, what exactly is a project? Sometimes it seems like the answer to everything at work.

'We need a new computer system.'
'*Let's set up a project to look at various systems.*'

or

'There's a problem with that production line.'
'*Let's get a project team together to suggest a solution.*'

Planning a project

Projects are usually about getting together a group of people to find a solution to a problem or to recommend how to do something. Project teams often involve people from different parts of the organization who each bring their own particular experience to the team. They can also be a group of people who already work together and have taken on one specific project task. As with school or college projects, there's usually a report at the end of the project – it doesn't have to be very long, and it shouldn't be complicated, as it's usually when the results (and recommendations, if there are any) are shared with colleagues outside the project team. And sometimes, you'll be asked to run a project on your own – in which case you'll probably need to work with relevant colleagues, to make sure you've got all the information and help you need.

Here are the main things to remember when planning a project:

● be clear about the project's aim or aims
● agree a realistic timescale
● do plenty of homework (time spent talking to relevant people early on can save time further down the line)
● get some support (your manager, another manager, a project team)
● if you're putting together a project team, make sure they'll all make a contribution (lots of people sign up, make no effort, then share any glory later!)

- start with a 'brainstorm' session to get all the possible issues written down. If it's just you working on the project, give yourself half an hour to jot down all the things you can think of (see p. 30 on 'think plan') and then talk it through with your manager or a colleague
- keep any paperwork simple! People cannot and will not spend ages reading sheets and sheets of paper. If you want their help, explain what you're doing and how – face to face if possible – answer any questions and follow up with a briefing note which sets out:

  – what the project aims to do
  – when it will be completed
  – what stages it will go through (such as research, consultation, drafting report, making presentation)
  – who's involved
  – who the main contact is (the project manager)
  – what you'd like from them (whether they're a project team member or not)
  – make sure you present the results in the right format and on time.

Managing a project

Here's a simple example of the kind of project plan you would have prepared if you'd been asked to move person A to another building and move person B into person A's old office.

Brainstorm (things to think about)
– what needs to be moved (all the furniture, all the files, any additional items) and from where to where?
– does A's office need cleaning or decorating before B moves in, and is the new office ready for A in the other building?
– when's the best time to move A and B's stuff?
– what happens to the phones?
– are there any health and safety risks?
– who needs to know before the move?
– how do I let everyone know after the move?
– who'll help them pack (if they need it)?
– what will they pack into?

Action list (drawn up from the brainstorm issues)

1   Check with A and B what they want to take, and make sure they know what's being left.
2   Check whether offices are OK – if not speak to maintenance manager about cleaning/painting/new lights, etc.
3   Produce floor plan and circulate to A and B, administration manager, customer services manager and maintenance manager.
4   Ask the customer services team to arrange for a Friday morning move out and to hold their stuff in a store room, so offices can be decorated on Friday afternoon and over the weekend, and cleaned on Monday morning. Need crates moved on Monday morning for unpacking by end of Monday.
5   Do note to administration manager regarding new phone numbers (they need eight working days' notice).
6   Contact maintenance team to check on any health and safety risks, and book Design Decorators from Friday midday and weekend (they need two weeks' notice).
7   Put a note on e-mail to let all the managers know about the move (three days' notice).
8   Put a note in the newsletter to let everyone know about the move (weekly newsletter – items in by Tuesday midday).
9   Visit A and B's current offices to estimate number of packing crates needed, then ask customer services to order from Rapid Removals (who need two weeks' notice).
10 Check when A and B are around to do their packing (Thursday afternoon or early Friday morning).
11 Write out project plan and send to A, B, customer services manager, administration manager and maintenance manager.

Now you've got a list of actions, you need to sort out a timetable for all the various activities – and slot the actions in (see overleaf). Start with your end-date or deadline and work backwards, building in the amount of notice everyone needs. Those sticky memo notes are ideal for planning your timetable as you can move them around until you're happy with it.

Timetable

Monday 20th	clean offices (2), A and B move in (3)
Weekend 18th, 19th	decorate
Friday 17th (by 1030)	move out – start to decorate (6)
Thursday 16th/early 17th	pack (1, 10)
Wednesday 15th	e-mail managers (7)
Tuesday 14th (by midday)	note into newsletter (8)
Tuesday 7th	note to admin manager (3, 5)
Monday 6th	agree moving arrangements with customer services (3, 4)
Friday 3rd	order crates (9)
Thursday 2nd	book decorators (6)
Wednesday 1st	visit offices (9) and draft floor plan (3) and project plan (11)

So your project plan to be sent round to those involved (11) would look like this:

Office moves – A and B

Co-ordinator: Jimmi (on extension 876)

When	*What*	*Who*
immediate	check everyone's details	Jimmi
Wednesday 1st	visit A and B's offices	Jimmi
	draft project plan and floor plan and send to A, B, admin manager, customer services manager, maintenance manager	Jimmi
Thursday 2nd	book decorators	Jimmi and maintenance manager
Friday 3rd	order crates	Jimmi and customer services manager

Monday 6th	agree moving arrangements	Jimmi and customer services and maintenance managers
Tuesday 7th	note about phones to admin manager	Jimmi
Tuesday 14th (midday)	note into newsletter	Jimmi
Wednesday 15th	e-mail to all managers	Jimmi
Thursday 16th / early 17th	pack crates	A and B
Friday 17th 1100–1200	(finish packing crates) crates into store	customer services and Rapid Removals
midday onwards	decorating (painting and putting up shelves)	Design Decorators
Saturday 18th (& Sunday 19th)	crates moved from store to new offices	customer services and Rapid Removals
	offices cleaned	Careful Cleaners
Monday 20th	Crates unpacked	A and B

Try and think about what might go wrong when you're planning (what if Rapid Removals aren't free on the 17th and 18th, what if A or B aren't around to pack on Thursday 16th or early on Friday 17th, what if Design Decorators pull out at the last minute, what if Careful Cleaners don't turn up, etc.?).

No matter how much planning you do, something will go wrong, but project management is about keeping calm and sorting things out! You know what it's like if you've spent weeks organising a get-together of friends and family and there's a train strike, motorway hold-up, the catering company lose your order and haven't done the food, the supermarket runs out of salad etc. etc.... It's frustrating and unlucky – but you find a way to cope.

The main guidelines are:
- be clear about aims and deadlines
- do your homework
- allow plenty of time for planning
- make sure you keep in touch with everyone who's involved or affected
- don't be afraid to ask for advice or help.

Point to remember
Projects are an important part of working life – in all areas and at all levels. The more experience you can get – as a project team member or as a project team manager – and the sooner you can get experience, the better.

Leadership

What kind of person inspires you? What kind of person would you follow in a battle or campaign?

Leadership is a strange thing. It's difficult to pin down what makes a good leader – of a country, an organization or a team – even though you know when you see a bad leader.

The interesting thing about most great leaders (politicians, campaigners, sports heroes) is that the people they lead and work with don't necessarily *like* them, but they respect them. Even the most frightening leaders, like dictators, appeal to and inspire people – although they may scare people into supporting them.

Organizations and teams need leaders *and* managers. Sometimes, the same people can be both, but there are major differences between the roles.

Managers need to be good at:

- planning
- controlling
- implementing policy
- sorting out resources
- administration
- getting results.

Leaders need to be good at:

● motivating
● making things possible
● mentoring
● communicating
● coming up with new ideas
● being energetic.

So leaders need to be good at guiding and inspiring other people, while managers need to be good at organizing and planning. Leaders may keep their focus on the bigger picture, while managers focus on shorter term goals.

The Industrial Society identified six key areas in which leaders need to be effective. It's worth remembering that good leaders don't have to be senior people, although most successful organizations do have a managing director or chief executive with good leadership skills. Supervisors, managers and project co-ordinators benefit from being good leaders too – and there are many great leaders throughout organizations. Here's what to look out for (and you can remember the areas by using the letters in the word 'leader').

L – **Liberates**: frees other people to do their best, gets rid of unnecessary barriers, makes things possible by:

● not blaming people
● encouraging people to take responsibility and decisions
● listening
● encouraging open communication
● developing trust, not suspicion
● encouraging ideas and creative thinking.

E – **Encourages and supports**: gives other people confidence and back-up by:

● accepting responsibility for what others do
● praising people where appropriate
● not letting people get stressed
● providing support
● meeting and listening to people
● showing confidence and faith in people.

A – **Achieves purpose**: gives other people a goal and sense of belief in themselves by:

- achieving results
- agreeing the right kinds of targets
- consulting people on decisions affecting them
- being prepared to take unpopular decisions
- looking for future challenges and opportunities
- inspiring people with a vision for the future
- looking for new ways to do things.

D – **Develops people and teams**: gives other people the chance to develop their talents and energies by:

- giving them chances to learn
- encouraging them to work together as a team
- having regular meetings to review progress
- developing and guiding other people
- tackling poor performance or bad behaviour
- treating mistakes as chances to learn and improve.

E – **Example-setting**: sets standards and provides a role model by:

- encouraging feedback on their own performance
- being enthusiastic
- learning new things themselves
- saying what they do and doing what they say
- owning up to mistakes
- setting an example for performance and behaviour.

R – **Relationship-builds**: earns people's trust, confidence and commitment by:

- not putting their own interests first
- keeping promises
- understanding people's feelings
- being calm under pressure and in a crisis
- being honest and truthful
- not taking credit for other people's successes
- being fair.

Point to remember
You can be a good leader without being a good manager – but really good managers are often good leaders too. If you ever have to manage something – a project or a team – then it's worth trying to make sure that you don't just manage but that you lead as well.

Managing your money

Everyone has difficult months – or years – as far as money goes. It can be especially difficult in the first year or so after starting work (or restarting after a long break) – whether your income goes up or down. Many people are on tight budgets, just about able to afford things they need without unexpected money problems. So if there is an unexpected bill or you need to make a major purchase, things can be difficult.

It's really important not to let money matters get you down. Keep a check on your expenditure and, if things are tight, do a monthly budget and stick to it. Here are the kinds of things you need to plan for (with essentials marked*):

- rent or mortgage *
- household bills *
- food and drink *
- clothes * (regular purchases like tights and socks as well as big items like a jacket and shoes including repairs)
- travel* (including petrol and servicing, if you have a car)
- general items (it's surprising how many odds and ends you can buy without even realising it – kitchen gadgets, a packet of fuses, batteries)
- hobbies/leisure/sport/music
- presents and cards (there's always someone with a birthday or anniversary)
- going out (food, drink, clubs, cinema, etc.)
- newspapers, magazines and books
- toiletries *
- haircut *
- loan repayments*/policy premiums*/subscriptions (magazines, membership fees, etc.)
- savings/holiday fund/emergency fund *.

Scary, isn't it? When you've made a list of your weekly or monthly expenditure, add it up – and compare it with your earnings. You're probably planning to spend more than you earn! So you need to manage you money until you earn a bit more and have a bit more to spend.

There are five things you can do to help manage your money.

- focus on essentials (marked ★ in the list above)
- give yourself regular treats so life doesn't feel completely miserable (it might be a trip to the cinema, a meal out, or even just a drink at a bar)
- plan your budget for each week or month, and watch your spending
- put a bit away whenever you can for emergencies and luxuries
- *never* let yourself get into deep financial trouble – it just makes everything worse.

Nobody really likes talking about money problems – whether it's to family, friends, your manager, or your bank. But it's better to get some help (and feel a bit embarrassed) rather than ending up in trouble. And don't take out expensive loans from dodgy individuals – they charge much higher interest rates than anywhere else and you'll be permanently in debt. Your family and friends might be able to help out in the short-term, just to tide you over. Everyone understands what it's like having to manage your money on top of everything else when you start a new job.

If you have a good working relationship with your manager, or your organization has a good HR person, then you could get advice from them. Some employers offer loans (often interest-free) to cover essential things like season tickets, and they may even be able to organize a short-term loan to help out with other things (you repay it out of your wages or salary over time). You can also try your bank – they often have advisers who can suggest various options. If they aren't helpful, then move your account elsewhere where you do get sensible advice.

Point to remember
Work and life are challenging enough without having money worries too. Always sort any money issues out before they become a real problem.

Basic skills

There are a few basic skills which everyone needs in order to cope with work and life. The essential four are:

Reading – being able to understand at least simple text for forms, noticeboards, general information and contracts, etc. In this country (the UK), English is the main language everyone needs to be able to understand.

Writing – being able to use basic words and sentences – writing clearly and spelling correctly, filling in forms, taking messages, writing letters and setting out information, etc. In this country, English is the main language everyone needs to be able to use.

You don't have to spell every word correctly (nobody can – that's what dictionaries are for). However, it's important to be able to spell basic and everyday words, plus any terms used regularly in your job or organization. As with many other subjects covered by this book, it's impossible to go into detail – it would be a book in itself – but here's a checklist of hints and tips.

● Make an effort to learn spellings you find difficult (test yourself).
● Look out for words that sound the same but are spelt differently (such as *brake* – on a car and *break* – split or fall apart).
● Read anything you've written back to yourself before sending it – check for spelling, sense and punctuation.
● Make sure you use punctuation correctly. Look out for:
  – full stops – end of sentence.
  – capital letters   **B**eginning of sentence
  – question mark – end of questions?
  – exclamation mark – end of surprised or amused comment!
  – commas – lists, splitting sentences into sections
  – speech marks (inverted commas) – 'quoting what someone says'
  – apostrophe – someone's punctuation
  – dashes – adding something – as an extra – to a sentence
  – brackets – adding something (same as dashes) to a sentence
  – hyphen – putting bits-and-pieces of words together

- semi-colon – there's one bit of a sentence; then there's another linked bit
- colon – used before: a list of items; a quotation or speech; a final statement
- paragraph – a short section in a piece of text (marked by a line gap between the sections).
- Try and pick up hints and tips on English grammar, remembering that:
  - a *noun* is a word that names something (*chair*)
  - an *adjective* is a word that describes a noun (*wooden* chair)
  - a *verb* is a doing word (*to sit, sitting*)
  - an *adverb* is a word that describes a verb (sitting *quietly*)
  - a *preposition* is a word that describes where/how things are in relation to other things (sitting quietly *in* the corner, *near* the chair).

If you know there are areas you need to brush up on, get a helpful book from the library (or buy one), or get help from a colleague who writes well. And remember spelling and grammar aren't just things you avoided at school – they can help you become an effective communicator – and communication is one of the most important skills you need for work.

Numbers – being able to use numbers for simple adding, subtracting, multiplying and dividing – as well as understanding percentages – for bills, budgets, pay slips and sales figures, etc.

Computers and calculators – being able to use keyboards, computers and word processors for on-screen information, paperwork, calculations, etc.

If you think you are not as confident in any of these areas as you'd like to be, then get some advice on how to build up your skills. It's nothing to be ashamed of – we're all better at some things than others! And everyone has to update their skills and learn new skills throughout their lives. Try your local college or training centre. Or speak to your HR or training officer, ask a colleague or friend to spend a few hours getting you started, look for books in your local library, or buy yourself a study book.

Other basic skills

- using the telephone effectively (and according to any organizational guidelines)
- using a photocopier (each one is different, and each one has its good and bad points – so learn about the one you have to use!)
- using a fax machine (always include a cover sheet)
- using a computer and printer – even if this isn't a key part of your job, you need to be able to use your organization's information systems (accounts, production management, etc.) and to produce simple documents
- using e-mail and the Internet (these are increasingly important communication methods).

Other useful skills

- speaking another language as well as English
- driving (very useful even if you don't own a car or need to drive regularly) including specialist or advanced driving (fork-lift trucks, HGVs, buses or trains, ambulances, etc.)
- cooking – don't laugh! We all need to be able to feed ourselves and to stay fit and healthy, so if you can't cook, try some basic recipes. You might get to enjoy it, and you can save money and improve your health.

Point to remember
Having good basic skills helps you get on in all areas of work and life. You can then build on them by developing other skills. It's always worth improving your basic skills if you aren't too confident about them.

Part Three

Your job

Your job

We all need goals to work towards – in life and at work. They partly give us a sense of direction, and they also help us know whether we're making any progress. Yes, it's great to wake up on a day off and know that you can please yourself all day, that you have no lists of things you have to do! But it's not much fun when every day's like that, because people are generally happier and feel better about themselves when they achieve things in life. Some of us are even high-energy people needing to get out and do things (painting a room, going for a session at the gym, weeding the garden, having a great evening out with friends, achieving something at work). Others are quite competitive, wanting to achieve new things all the time or more than other people.

People who for some reason can't get out, or do, as much as they'd like can sometimes feel frustrated or even useless. So, however bad you might feel about having to get up and go to work – remember that there are lots of benefits (income, social contact, a sense of purpose and achievement).

Job targets

You should have some sort of job description for your job, which usually sets out the main activities you are required to do and some additional things you may have to do from time to time. It might look like this:

Job: team administrator
Key activities:

- handling post, phone calls, e-mail and diaries for three team consultants
- word processing consultants' paperwork (letters, memos, etc.)
- attending consultants' meetings with clients to provide administrative input
- project managing consultants' projects
- acting as a contact point for other teams and departments.

Additional activities:

- contributing to other teams' projects where appropriate
- briefing consultants on technology updates (word processors, telephones, etc.)
- organizing team 'away days'.

You should also have some guidelines on performance and outputs – specific to your job. For example, this team administrator job might have the following:

Key activity 1: handling post, etc.
Performance measures:

- post opened within half an hour of delivery – either actioned, filed or flagged up for consultants' attention
- phone used according to guidelines (see telephone manual). All messages recorded in the message book
- e-mail monitored hourly – or when messages are highlighted – and either actioned, printed off for filing, or passed to consultants for information/action.

Key activity 2: word processing, etc.
Performance measures:

- paperwork produced according to house style manual guidelines. All drafts produced within deadline agreed with consultants.

Key activity 3: attending meetings, etc.
Performance measures:

- notes to be taken at consultants' meetings and circulated to clients and consultants
- client file to be taken to every meeting and any administrative issues relating to client contact flagged up.

Key activity 4: project managing, etc.
Performance measures:

- project management to be within team guidelines (see team's project manual).

Key activity 5: acting as contact point, etc.
Performance measures:

- all other teams to be visited at least monthly (book ten minute visits when convenient) to update their administrator on our team's priorities and progress, and to hear their news
- monthly team administrator meetings to be attended.

You'll see that these kinds of guidelines give you a framework to work within, and they also give your manager a framework for measuring how you're doing in the job. For example, if you aren't producing documents according to the house style guidelines (2) your manager can raise this with you, or if you aren't attending the monthly team meetings (5) your boss can check why.

Competencies

Sometimes organizations use the word 'competencies' linked to performance and skills development. It's another way of saying 'things people can do', and it is used to explain what skills and abilities people need to have in order to do their job. Using the example job on p. 76 the competencies might be:

- time management
- project planning and management
- written communication
- typing and proof-reading documents
- building relationships with colleagues and customers
- understanding and using technology.

Performance targets

Performance targets give you something to aim for in your job. Targets at work or in life should be challenging – there's no point in having targets you can easily reach because it gets boring and there's no real sense of achievement – but they should be achievable. There's no point in having targets which you're never going to achieve either, because you'll get fed up and feel a bit of a failure all the time.

So your performance targets need to be a mixture of:

● things directly linked to your everyday job
● new things that will make you (and sometimes your colleagues) more effective
● training and learning new skills
● personal development.

You should do some thinking about possible targets, but your manager should also have some ideas, so you can come up with a good list between you. Sometimes your manager might get you to agree to a target that scares you. If you really think it's unreasonable then say so, and agree to something you're more comfortable with. This is particularly important if some of your pay (performance-related pay) depends on achieving your targets. But remember that your manager will be wanting you to do as well as you possibly can, and they may have more confidence in you than you do in yourself! So it's about finding a balance between challenging (something that will take effort and will develop you) and unreasonable (something you'll never get to, even if you were working 24 hours a day). It's not fair, either, for managers to put people under unnecessary pressure all the time as this can lead to stress, illness and, sometimes, under-performance – when people just get so tired and fed up, they give up.

On the other hand, you might want to set targets that scare your manager! You may be aiming really high, and they may be worried that you'll put yourself under too much pressure. Remember – no matter how confident you feel, your manager may be giving you good advice and they may be trying to help you perform well without overstretching yourself. Don't try to set too many high targets. It might seem brave to have a list of 32 – but that's difficult to keep track of, and you probably won't be able to focus on any main aims as you'll have so many smaller targets to worry about. Also, it can just make you feel like you're on overload. Depending on your job, your team and the type of targets you go for, between 4 and 12 is usually a manageable number.

Always include at least one personal development target.

If your organization doesn't help you set targets for your job (they just expect you to get on with it) then you should sit down and work out your own list of targets – perhaps a mixture of work and personal objectives. Then you can measure how well you're doing and get a sense of progress.

Performance problems

Sometimes a person's performance problems will take more then just a bit of advice from their manager to solve.

There's a difference between *not being able to do* something (lacking skills or ability) and *not doing* something (because you don't care or don't bother).

If a manager talks things through with somebody – offers help, gives a timescale for improvement – and there's still a problem with the employee's performance, then it's usually time for the disciplinary process.

Discipline doesn't mean punishing someone, but it does mean getting someone back onto the right track. It's a formal way of saying that there is a problem and that the person involved needs to sort it out.

Disciplinary processes usually include (in this order):

- verbal warnings
- final warnings
- dismissal
- appeal.

Organizations should not just dismiss (sack, fire) someone straight off for a performance problem (not meeting sales targets, being rude to a customer, turning up late for work) without trying some performance management ideas (using 1:1 meetings to spot and solve problems, offering training, changing the job, etc.) – for two reasons. First, because it often takes only one bit of action to solve a problem and keep a good, committed person in the organization. Second, because in the UK the law says you can't just get rid of people without going through all the relevant procedures unless they have done something really terrible (beating up a colleague, stealing large amounts of money, etc.) in which case you can omit the warning process and suspend the individual until the incident has been investigated.

Finally, sometimes a performance problem can be solved by moving someone from one job to another in the organization, or by letting them change the hours they work. People sometimes just end up in the wrong job – or they have too much to cope with at certain times in their lives. They may be hardworking and skilled employees who are worth keeping – but they need to move elsewhere within the organization.

Performance management through 1:1 meetings

Many organizations have a way of monitoring and reviewing people's performance. It usually means regular 1:1 meetings, often monthly, with your manager – where you go over what's happened since you last met, you agree on priorities for the next few weeks or months, you discuss any possible problems, and you explain how you feel you're getting on. You should prepare for a 1:1 performance/progress meeting by thinking about which bits of your job are going well, and where there are any difficulties or things you find challenging. Check back against your job description and performance targets each time you get ready for this kind of meeting, and jot down a few helpful notes to remind yourself of what you want to talk about in the meeting. Your manager should have prepared for the 1:1 meeting by checking the file containing notes from your previous meetings and making a note of any issues they want to discuss.

This kind of meeting is when your manager should raise any performance issues with you (*'I'm concerned that you seem to be missing project management deadlines'*, etc.) and agreeing any actions to help you improve your performance if necessary. This may occasionally lead to the disciplinary process. You should use this kind of meeting to mention any issues to do with your own performance (*'I'm really pleased that I seem to be beating all the project management deadlines'* or *'I feel I'm not confident enough when I…'*) as well as raising any difficult issues with your manager if appropriate (such as problems with colleagues). You can also use these meetings to ask for time off, book your holiday or explain any problems in your personal life that might be affecting your performance at work (*'I'm afraid my sister is really ill at the moment, so I'm having some trouble concentrating'* or *'I may need to take a few days off this month as the children are on school holiday and the play scheme I usually use is shut one day a week'*).

The 1:1 meeting should take between 20 minutes and an hour, depending on how much you usually need to discuss together.

Your manager should send you a copy of their notes soon after the meeting, so you're both clear about what was agreed and any specific points raised. If you don't think the notes are right (the wrong date for a deadline or something you didn't agree to) then talk to your manager and sort things out.

Appraisal

You should have one major meeting (usually once a year) called the 'appraisal', when you go back over your performance for the whole year (since your last annual appraisal) and plan your performance targets for the year ahead. If you have one appraisal each year, its best if you and your manager use your 1:1 meetings every three months to review performance in particular.

You and your manager should both think about your appraisal beforehand, and go over the notes for the year's 1:1 meetings. Both of you should also look at your job description, any team targets, what your organization *needs* everyone to do, and what it's *encouraging* everyone to do (often linked to the organizational 'mission' or goals, and where you could develop your skills – at and outside work – which you'd enjoy and which would benefit your organization. You should spend around a third of your appraisal meeting talking about the past year (sheets 1 and 2) and two-thirds setting targets for the future (sheet 3), in these sorts of areas:

● any new responsibilities to add to the job, plus performance measures
● how you can help the rest of the team
● what personal development you can do – within the organization and outside.

Your appraisal should look something like this:

Sheet 1: review of 1998–1999			
Key job activities	**Performance measures**	**Target**	**Appraisal review**
1. Post, phone, e-mail diaries	– post opened and actioned promptly – phone used in line with guidelines – all messages noted – all e-mail collected and actioned promptly	– get all consultants onto e-mail by end October – get 20% of clients using e-mail not post by mid-January	Done Done
2. Paperwork, word-processing, etc.	etc.	etc.	etc.
6. Skills development, training, learning new skills, developing knowledge	– competence to do job increases – frees up time to do other things and develop job	– go on advanced WP course by October – join internal project management team (immediate)	Done Ongoing
7. Personal development – learning new skills outside work	– personal confidence increases – network of contacts expands	– volunteer to help at youth club once a month – do Spanish evening classes	Ongoing Done

Sheet 2: job competencies				
	Shows competence (tick box)			
	Always	**Usually**	**Occasionally**	**Never**
Time management	✓			
Project planning and management	✓			
Written communication		✓		
Typing and proof-reading documents		✓		
Building relationships with colleagues and customers			✓	
Understanding and using technology		✓		

Sheet 3: Performance measures and targets for 1999–2000			
Key job activities	**Performance measures**	**Target**	**Appraisal review**
1. Post, phone, e-mail diaries	– post opened and actioned promptly – phone used in line with guidelines – all messages noted – all e-mail collected and actioned promptly	– set up electronic diary system for yourself by end July, for manager and consultants by end October – renegotiate express parcel delivery contract – either improve with exisiting company or select new one who offer better deal	
7. Personal development – learning new things outside work	– personal confidence increases – network of contacts expands	– do Italian evening evening classes – join charity committee	

Feedback

Some organizations will not only get views on your performance from you and your manager (and sometimes your manager's manager) but they will also collect feedback from a range of people you work with elsewhere in the organization (and occasionally even outside it). This all-round appraisal is called '360 degree appraisal'. In the example job, the job holder's manager could send the following sheet to one of the consultants, another team administrator, another manager who's worked with this job holder on a project, and a client who deals regularly with the team administrator.

Sheet 4: 360 degree appraisal feedback form

CONFIDENTIAL

As part of our all-round appraisal process, I would be grateful if you could complete this form and return it to me in the stamped, addressed envelope provided. Many thanks.

Manager's name, job title, department and organization:

Your name, job title, department and organization:

1. Comments on job holder's:

–   communication skills

–   project and time management

–   paperwork/document standards

–   relationship with you

2. Any other comments on job holder's skills and job performance

3. Any other comments which might be useful in the appraisal process

If you are asked to give some feedback on another colleague's performance remember to be clear, be fair and focus on what the person does and how they do it – don't get personal. If you're giving written feedback:

- include positive feedback wherever possible.
- keep it short using any forms provided, typed if possible
- make it clear what you mean, don't hint at things
- explain any problems or difficult issues

If you're giving verbal feedback:

- use the communication guidelines in Part Two to get your points across
- be prepared to answer any questions about your feedback – don't get defensive.

Remember that you need to agree to all your targets, you need to talk through all the performance issues and your manager should explain where they have any concerns about your competence. Don't worry if your appraisal sheets look different from these examples – every organization has a different approach (there may be extra or fewer sheets) but the content is usually roughly the same:

- what you have to do in your job (linked to your job description)
- how you have to do it (linked to performance and competencies) and what you're aiming to do (targets linked to what your team needs you to do and what your organization needs you to do)
- how well you've done in various areas and overall.

And remember – an appraisal meeting should always be a mixture of positive and negative things – and you should always get a copy of the completed sheets for your own file (sheet 5).

Sheet 5: Appraisal comments 1998–1999

Job holder's comments

Manager's comments

Signed off by (usually your manager's manager)

Sheet 6: performance bonus recommendations

Job holder's name:

Their job title and department:

Manager's name and job title:

Performance for [year] (copies of sheets 1 to 5 attached)

outstanding   excellent   good   fair   poor
                      ✓

Performance bonus recommendation: 1   ②   3   4

Signed off by the manager's manager

Performance-related pay

Many organizations link the 'how well you've done' bit (the appraisal review column on sheet 1) to any performance awards or bonuses – lump sums or pay increases. So it's not only important to do your job well so you *feel* good about it, but also because it may *do* you some good – through your pay packet. There can be another sheet like this (sheet 6 on p. 87).

Pay and benefits

Most people want to earn money. Yes, there are lots of other reasons why people work – and money isn't everyone's top priority – but it's a key reason for most of us. That means money's an important issue at work.

Very few of us feel we're paid enough! Some people think they should earn more because of the hours they put in or the value of what they do, and others feel underpaid compared to others in their organization and other organizations. There is no national pay scale in the UK – in fact, there are regional differences – and there is no upper limit on what people can be paid (remember the stories about 'fat cats'?). But there are some general patterns within sectors or job types (because the organizations have to pay somewhere near the 'going rate' otherwise good candidates wouldn't appy to work with them). In the UK there is a National Minimum Wage (with the hourly rate set by the Low Pay Commission and reviewed annually). However, some variations from the National Minimum Wage will be allowed (for example, people aged 18 to 21).

Pay

Your 'gross' pay is your total pay before any amounts have been deducted. Items that might come out of your pay include:

- contributions to National Insurance (UK) or social welfare – the contribution can be payable by both employer and employee
- income taxes (at different levels depending on your rate of pay) which your employer may be legally obliged to send to the government

- pension contributions, if you've signed up to join a pension scheme run by your employer
- loan repayments – if you've taken out a season ticket or study loan, for example
- medical insurance premiums.

Your 'net' pay is what remains after any such deductions and it's what gets paid into your bank account or handed over to you at the end of the week or month.

How are pay rates decided by an employer? Well, there are at least five factors which can affect an organization's pay system:

- job holder's range of activities and levels of responsibilities
- scarce or specialist skills
- what's happened before
- sector or job 'norms'
- law.

Let's have a look at these factors.

Activities and responsibilities

If an organization wants to be fair about how it pays people it should have some sort of system which groups similar jobs together so that people doing jobs of roughly the same 'size' and 'level' get paid about the same amount. This is usually known as a 'job evaluation' system. Some of these systems can be incredibly (and unnecessarily) complicated, often bought from consultants who like to make themselves look clever. But, put simply, a job evaluation system scores every job against an agreed list of key activities and levels of responsibility. So jobs with lots of different activities each involving quite a lot of responsibility score higher than jobs involving only a few main activities and very little responsibility. Higher scoring jobs fall into higher pay bands, and lower scoring jobs into lower pay bands. Pay bands are set according to a mixture of the following four factors.

Scarce or specialist skills

If your organization needs to employ people with scarce or specialist skills they may find it difficult to attract the right people unless they pay above the standard (or job evaluation) pay rate –

temporarily, or in the long term (for example, with computer experts). This can mess up a job evaluation system.

What's happened before

Unfortunately, some organizations have pay systems based on many different decisions taken in the past. This can mean that some employees are underpaid for what they do, and others are overpaid. It can cause bad feeling, not surprisingly. The main example of this is that jobs traditionally done by women can be undervalued compared to similar kinds of jobs (in terms of the range of activities and level of responsibilities) done by men in that organization or sector.

Sector or job 'norms'

There are some sectors or types of job which are traditionally better or worse paid than others (even though, when you think about it, the sector or job has a lot in common with others). One example is nurses and people working in public sector care services, who tend to be paid less than other people in service industries – even though they have a similar type and level of responsibility.

Law

As mentioned on page 88, in the UK there is a National Minimum Wage. There are several other UK laws to do with pay, including the Equal Pay Act and the Employment Rights Act 1996 Part II.

Extra pay and benefits

Items which may be added to normal starting pay include:

- overtime payment – usually paid at one and a half or double your regular pay rate
- bonus – usually a one off amount added when you've done really well at work
- performance award – a percentage increase on your salary or a one-off bonus after you've done really well at work
- pay rise – percentage increase, usually at the same time each year, and often linked to how much the cost of living has gone up

- promotion – if you get promoted to a new job you'll probably get a pay increase – it may not be much, but every bit's worth having
- profit-share – people who are 'partners' in profit-making organizations get an amount as their share of profits
- profit-related pay – a few organizations in the UK pay part of employees' earnings (usually no more than 5%) linked to how well the organization has done (it can be nothing in bad years, but you can do well in good years)
- performance-related pay – some organizations pay part of employees' earnings based on each employee's performance (so, if you've done really well, you get paid a lot)
- London (or regional) allowance – employers often have to pay an allowance to get and keep employees in certain areas – cities or remote places, for example – or working abroad
- vouchers – some people get vouchers for food or childcare – on top of their basic pay
- car or petrol allowance – some organizations provide a car – (usually up to a maximum price) or offer a car or petrol allowance
- membership – providing sports or leisure centre facilities or membership, or paying for membership of professional clubs, associations
- medical insurance – you may choose to pay for this out of your earnings through a scheme run by your employer, or your employer may even cover you
- you may get a subsidy from your employer to cover study fees or the cost of an exam course.

Some of these things are taxed (at various rates) because the government sees them as financial benefits in addition to your pay. Check what's what, so you understand how much you're getting and how much you're paying out. You need to keep records of any additional pay or job benefits you get on top of your basic pay – for tax reasons. And if you have two or more jobs, you need to keep records of all your pay and benefits, to make sure you pay the right amount of tax.

You also need to check whether your employer will let you swap any extra benefits for another benefit or for cash instead. This is sometimes called a 'cafeteria' benefits system (because it's like picking and choosing what you want for lunch). For example, you might want to swap your car allowance for childcare vouchers.

The main things to remember about pay are:

● check your pay slips and query them if they don't look right
● keep records for at least three years (UK)
● answer any tax queries straight away
● ask the relevant person in your organization (HR, payroll, etc.) if your think there may be a mistake
● keep a look out for legal ways of earning a bit more.

Pensions

Don't turn over – this isn't an advert! Pensions aren't about being old – they are a way of saving regularly during your working life to make sure you have a pot of money to live on when you stop. It's really important that you start putting a bit of your income towards your pension as early as possible in your working life, because any state pension may not be enough to live on comfortably.

In the UK there are three main ways of saving towards your pension:

● occupational pension scheme – run by your employer, who will sometimes pay a bit on your behalf
● personal pension scheme – run by a financial services or insurance company
● additional voluntary contibutions (AVCs) – extra top-up payments on top of your usual pension payments.

Most of us will end up with a mixture of different bits to our pension, collected as we change jobs and circumstances over our lives. And in the UK a new type of pension is being developed, called a 'stakeholder' pension, which is meant to make sure that everyone has a decent income during their retirement.

Pensions sound really complicated. But, put simply, a pension is just like a savings account which you can't touch until you retire. The money you put in over the years is invested on your behalf, so – if it's properly looked after (and safely invested) – it should provide a decent pot of money which is then often used when you retire to pay out regular monthly amounts for you to live on.

There are some problems with pensions (there are often problems when people manage other people's money) but you can help protect your pension plan by:

- reading all the paperwork before you sign up
- getting advice (from the pensions person in your organization, an employee representative, or an approved independent financial adviser) if you're not sure about what to choose or don't understand some of the details
- joining an employer's scheme if you can, especially if it's got a good track record.

If all else fails, open a savings account anyway and try to save up to 10% of your pay every month – which you can later invest in a pension when you finally choose one. You may be able, in the UK, to use one of the new Individual Savings Accounts (ISAs) for starting off your savings.

Point to remember
Always check your pay and benefits statements, and keep a record of what you earn for at least three years. And start saving towards your pension as soon as you start work.

Management

We all have to manage as part of our jobs (even if our job titles don't officially say 'manager'). We have to manage our time and various resources in order to do our jobs effectively. Some of us may also have to manage projects, teams, departments or organizations.

One helpful way to look at management is to think of the five different directions in which you need to manage. They are:

- Managing upwards – almost everyone has a manager, and you need to be able to work with yours.
- Managing downwards – we're all responsible for managing various resources – equipment, materials, money, time, work areas and information – in order to do our job. Sometimes you may also be responsible for managing people – either a full-time team or people working with you on a project.

- Managing across the organization – it's vital for everyone in an organization to build strong links with colleagues throughout the organization. You need trust and good communication to help everyone to do their job well and fit in with everyone else's activities.
- Managing outside the organization – most of us have regular contact with people outside our organization – whether it's customers, suppliers, contractors, visitors or general callers. For some of us it's a big part of our jobs, and for others it happens occasionally.
- Managing yourself – we all have to manage our time, our skills, our moods and our stress levels. And managing ourselves also includes working out how much time and effort to put into the other four management directions. You don't need to split your time evenly between all five, but you do need to decide on your priorities – and be careful not to put too much into one direction at the expense of another.

Here's a reminder of the management 'compass', before we look at some guidelines for each direction.

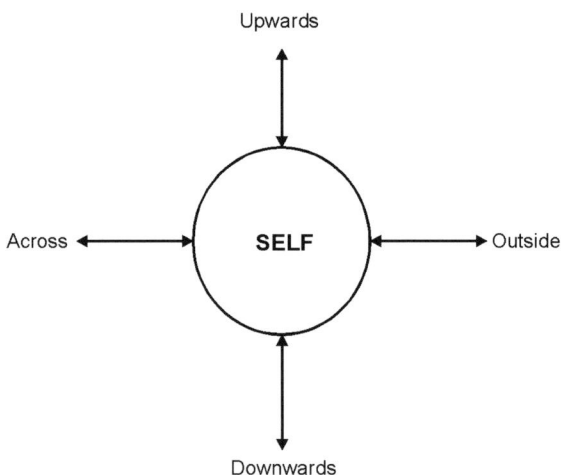

Managing upwards

Make sure you:

- understand your manager's job (what's written down is sometimes different from what really goes on)

- work out where your job ends and where your manager's begins
- sort out any overlaps (there's more than enough to do without two people trying to do the same tasks)
- meet regularly to update each other on progress, problems and priorities
- agree where you can take any tasks away from your manager (you might have more skills or time than they do) and where you need help from them
- learn by watching and listening – sometimes how to do things, sometimes how not to do things
- prepare in advance if you have to deal with other managers, not just your own (passing on information, making a presentation, etc.)
- keep a look out for any development opportunities – you may not want or be able to move into your manager's job, but you may pick up ideas on where to go next
- remember that your manager has a different set of priorities, so if you want to explain something, you need to think about the issue from their point of view and explain it from that angle
- take any opportunities to 'workshadow' your manager, following them for a day or two to learn about their job.

Managing downwards

Make sure you:

- are clear about what resources you've got to do your job (sometimes people forget to tell you)
- make a list of all your physical resources (equipment, materials, money, work areas) and check to see whether you need anything else to do your job properly
- do your homework – if you need to ask for more or new resources, remember to make some notes about what you want, why you want it, how much it will cost and what the benefits will be
- plan how you're going to use your time and keep checking that things are getting done by relevant deadlines, if not, you'll have to change the way you're working in some way

- have all the information you need to do your job (ever wondered why something seems really hard to do – and then you discover you're missing a vital bit of information or some simple instruction?)
- are developing as many management skills as possible – even if responsibilities seem scary now, the more you do the more you will learn, and it usually gets easier with practice
- are clear about what to do if you're managing people or projects. Any people you manage need:
  i)   clear targets and deadlines
  ii)   a clear explanation of what's needed
  iii) support and guidance
  iv)   regular communication (two-way – you talk to them, they feed back to you)
  v)   freedom to get on with things as much as possible
  vi)   recognition for what they're doing
  vii) thanks and praise for doing a good job
  viii) enjoyment for being part of a team – even if it's only a team of two – you and them.

Other aspects of managing downwards include:

● Any projects you manage (sometimes just you, often involving other people) need to be planned and co-ordinated using the guidelines on p. 59.
● Don't dump everything on others – or take on everything yourself. Try this quick way of checking how you're spreading the load:

	Recommend	Act	Pass on
Task			

For each task, check whether you should be asking your manager's view before making a decision (recommend), just getting on with it (act) or getting someone else to take action (pass on). The **RAP** check is a handy way of sorting out who's managing what, and of making sure you're not overloaded (and that you're not passing too much stuff on to others either).

- Remember that when you explain things to people or ask them to do something, you need to tell them what, when, how and why (and sometimes where). For example, here are four different versions of an e-mail to a colleague working with you on a project:
- — *Please could you make a list [by turnover] of our top ten customers. Thanks.* (what).
- — *Please, by this Friday, could you make a list [by turnover] of our top ten customers. Thanks.* (what and when).
- — *Please could you make a list [by turnover] of our top ten customers, using the 1997-98 accounts figures, and get it to me by this Friday. Thanks.* (what, when and how).
- — *Please could you make a list [by turnover] of our top ten customers, using the 1997-1998 accounts figures, and get it to me by this Friday. My manager needs it for the sales meeting next Tuesday. Thanks.* (what, when, how and why).

You'll see that the last one would make you want to help (you don't need a 'where' here) but the first one could make you think '*I'll do it when I have time*' or '*I won't bother until they chase me*'.

- Don't breathe down people's necks all the time! Managing isn't about checking up or even spying on people. It's about getting the most out of who and what are available to do the job.
- Identify problems as early as possible by keeping in touch with what's going on and the people involved. If you're managing an activity, a project or people you are responsible for getting the results. So if things are going slowly or going wrong, you need to sort it out by working out what the problem is and putting it right (it might be lack of resources, people's lack of confidence or skills, or a hold-up beyond your control).
- Be prepared to take any difficult decisions when you need to (one of the worst things about management). For example, say you are put in charge of a project and asked to get two colleagues to work with you on it. One of your friends at work is really keen to get involved but you don't feel they have the right skills to help get the project done successfully and on time. Are you prepared to explain this to them (see p. 35 for advice on assertiveness and p. 18 for advice on

communication skills) and to choose someone else with the right skills? Not easy!

● Don't hang on until you have every last bit of information you need before making every single decision. Trust your instincts and use your skills and experience whenever possible.

Managing across the organization

Make sure you:

- know who you need to know. In a small organization (say, up to a dozen people) you can network with everyone – and you probably need to work as one big team. But in a larger organization you need to manage proactive and reactive contacts effectively (the people you make contact with and the people who contact you) because you can't possibly get to know everyone and their jobs

- remember that what people hear from you is what they'll think about you and your team colleagues. So a positive and helpful response to a query says good things about you – and you will find it easier to work with them if you need to. But a negative or unhelpful response will give a bad impression of you – and you will find it difficult to work with them if you need to in the future

- find out which people to get in touch with across your organization – people who can help you do your job more effectively. For example, if you're in a customer service role in a shop, you need to get on with the department managers and the cleaners – as they all help you solve customers' problems at various times

- are as helpful as you can be and return favours! Remember a few personal details about the people you deal with in your organization. Colleagues tend to respond better if you treat them like a person, not just as a source of information. For example: *'Hi Pete! How are you? ... Good – and how are the children? ... Great! Anyway, I wondered if you could give me some advice on ...'* is much more effective than: *'Hi Pete! I need your help with ...'* Wouldn't you like to be on the receiving end of the first example, rather than the second?

- understand that different teams work in different ways and to different timescales. For example, it isn't necessarily rude if someone you've called asks you to call back later or the next day if they have an urgent priority (cashing up or dealing with a customer order or meeting a deadline for some typing)

- remember that other people are also managing their time and resources – so managing across the organization is about finding ways of helping each other get the job done, being flexible and co-operative

- agree 'ground rules' at the start if you're working on a project with colleagues – you don't want to have to keep sorting out priorities and planning time on top of actually doing the project work

- look out for any sideways development opportunities. As many organizations are 'flatter' these days (see p. 5) there aren't as many opportunities as there used to be for promotion. But you might find a way to move on in another team through working with various colleagues across the organization

- use contacts across the organization as a chance to learn. Don't yawn when someone says 'Shall I just explain what we do?' – listen. It's amazing how useful those bits of background information can be

- plan and use your time effectively. We could all spend our time at work chatting to people around the organization about how to get something done – and then never actually do it! Remember that managing your links across the organization is about helping you do your job or complete a project – not about preventing you from doing it

- note down useful information and details – for your own reference or to get agreement from the person you're in touch with on how you'll work together

- don't make promises you can't keep. Don't say 'yes' to a suggestion or request if you can't handle it or if the deadline's too tight. It's about getting the job done, not about taking on as many jobs as possible (some people do that to make themselves look and feel important – but they regret it in the end when they either miss deadlines, do lots of things not very well or make themselves ill from overwork)

- use any relevant ways of getting and keeping in touch with people across the organization. There's nothing to beat face to face discussions where possible – especially when you first

start working with people – but it's often quicker to keep things moving using e-mail, phone calls, memos – depending on what you need to communicate. Posters on noticeboards also work if you're wanting to attract colleagues' attention or get support – and items in your organization's newsletter can also be a good way of reaching people across the organization
– keep this sort of management under control.

Managing outside the organization

Make sure you:
– also keep this area under control. You may have dozens or even hundreds of regular contacts outside the organization, and you could spend 24 hours a day just keeping in contact with them, let alone doing your job
– work out who are your key contacts in these three areas:
    i) *no choice*: external people you have to deal with. For example, if you work in a postroom, it will include the postal authorities; if you work in an accounts department, it may include the tax authorities; and if you work in a factory, it may include health and safety inspectors
    ii) *some choice*: external people you generally have to be aware of and in touch with, but you have some flexibility about who and when. For example, if you work in a press office you might choose to keep in closer touch with one local newspaper rather than another; if you work in a sales team you might contact a few customers regularly to tell them about special offers; and if you work in a call-centre you might keep in touch with someone from a similar local business to keep them up to date and hear news from their organization – so you both benefit
    iii) *free choice*: external people whose information or advice can help you do your job better, and who like hearing from you. For example, if you're responsible for stationery orders, you might keep in touch with one or two suppliers who tend to give you a good deal; if you work in an oil refinery, you might keep in touch with someone you know from another local industry, to swap views on jobs and industry developments; and if you work as a secretary, you might keep in touch with an administrator from

another company (someone you met through a training course or socially) to hear about what's going on in your field elsewhere.

All three types of contact – however much choice you have over them – should help you do your job better in some way. It's always useful to have an outside view on things, and it can help solve problems.

– know that external contacts fall broadly into the following categories, and you need to manage each group differently:

   i) *customers:* it's generally true that 80% of an organization's profits come from the top 20% of their customers. In profit-making organizations, customers keep you in business. In non-profit making organizations, your customers are the people who use your services, so without them your organization wouldn't exist

   ii) *suppliers:* it isn't usually a good idea to keep changing suppliers, often just to save money. It's more important to build strong links with them, so they want to provide a good service and you can rely on them

   iii) *local and general government:* the decisions your local authority takes may have an important effect on your organization, and so will central government's policies and laws. So any contacts you have can be helpful in making sure you're prepared for changes

   iv) *community:* wherever your organization is based there will be many people and other organizations who can affect what you do and who are affected by what your organization does. It's much better to be in touch with them and work with them wherever appropriate. And future employers are out there too

   v) *competitors:* it's not just about beating them, it's also vital to learn from them – their successes and mistakes – and sometimes to work in partnership with them

   vi) *media:* it's important to give a positive message about your organization. You may occasionally come into contact with newspaper, TV and radio journalists wanting information about your organization. The important thing is not to give any information (unless you're the press officer, of course) and to know which of your colleagues deals with these kinds of queries.

Managing yourself

You're not meant to panic after reading the previous four sections! They're meant to give you a feel for the different aspects of management in an organization, but the most important thing is for you to manage yourself so you can do your own job effectively. Make sure you:

— understand your job's targets
— know where you fit into your team and the organization
— ask questions if you're not clear about what's expected of you or about what resources you have
— plan how you're going to use your time
— work out if there are changes you can make which will help you do your job better. Make sure you're spending enough time managing up, down, across and outside – but not too much
— have regular 1:1 meetings with your manager, to keep an eye on what's going on and get ideas and advice on any problems
— work to build up any links which you need to help you do your job better
— think about new ways of doing your job – which might make it quicker or easier
— don't always leave the things you like least or are not as good at until last (or, worse, not do them at all)
— look for opportunities to develop your skills (or learn new ones) beyond your job. You are responsible for managing your personal development
— manage your stress levels – by planning your workload, using your time effectively, keeping a balance between work and home and keeping fit and healthy.

Point to remember
Management is a balancing act. Sometimes it seems as though no matter what you do or how well you plan, things don't go right in your job. And solving that kind of

'bad day' problem is just another aspect of management. So being able to manage in five different directions, as and when needed, is an important part of being able to survive at work – and of getting the most out of your job.

Health & safety

In the UK everyone is responsible for health and safety in the workplace. You need to make sure that you're working safely and that you don't put anyone else at risk. There are many danger areas in workplaces, ranging from everyday items like things left on the floor, which people can trip over, to complicated things like chemicals, which may be lethal when spilt or inhaled.

Health and safety covers a wide range of issues – including:

- eyestrain from using a computer screen too long without a break or focusing on text or small objects
- minor injuries – cuts and bruises
- headaches due to stuffy or noisy rooms
- eardrum damage from high-pitched or loud noises
- strained or damaged arms, wrists and fingers from using keyboards or machine tools
- strained or damaged necks, backs and legs from sitting incorrectly for too long or from lifting heavy weights
- lung, mouth, skin and eye damage from chemicals
- burns due to fire or explosion
- loss of limbs or serious injury due to falls, being caught in machinery or being run over
- violence caused by colleagues, customers or service-users
- various injuries caused by car crashes (driving a company vehicle)
- infection transmitted by food, air or blood-to blood contact
- injuries due to getting hair or clothes caught in moving machinery (from photocopiers through to factory machines)
- nerve damage, caused by repeated vibration (from a drilling tool, etc.)
- stress-related illness caused by too much work, too little time, too few resources or too much worrying (about family responsibilities, illness, etc.).

There are three main aspects of health and safety:

● laws and regulations – in the UK the Health and Safety at Work Act 1974 covers employers, employees, self-employed people, contractors, supporters and non-workers affected by other people's work. Other major laws include: Control of Substances Hazardous to Health Regulations 1998; Consumer Protection Act 1987; Electricity at Work Regulations 1989; Noise at Work Regulations 1989; Offices, Shops and Railway Premises Act 1963; Reporting of Injuries, Diseases and Dangerous Occurrences Regulations 1985, and the 1992 EU six-pack
● your employer's own rules and regulations
● your common-sense approach to doing your job safely.

Laws and regulations

All laws are complicated, but employers have to get to grips with them. There are UK guidelines (called Guidance Notes and Codes of Practice) which help employers make sense of health and safety law and explain what they should and shouldn't do. The law acknowledges that you can't get rid of every hazard all the time – workplaces are busy places – but it requires employers to do what is 'reasonably practicable' to prevent accidents at work. Your employer should be making regular checks (sometimes called 'audits') on the key factors, taking action where necessary. Some of your colleagues may even be trained as health and safety representatives, fire marshals or first-aiders – a role which people often agree to adopt in addition to their job. If there is an accident – however small – the following should happen:

● those involved are given any help or treatment they need
● the incident is reported in the accident book (it's worth finding out where this is kept in your organization)
● the appropriate person (HR officer, employee representative or health and safety representative, for example) reviews what happened and why, and works out what should be done to avoid it happening again.

If there is a serious accident, there will have to be an external investigation by a national or state authority (in the UK, the Health and Safety Executive which monitors and sets health and safety standards). They will want to find out whether:

- the employer had taken all reasonable steps to review health and safety standards, train and inform employees, set up health and safety procedures and provide relevant safety equipment to prevent accidents
- employees had caused the accident by careless, dangerous or foolish behaviour
- it was a genuine accident, which couldn't be prevented.

If an employer or employee is found to have caused an accident (directly – by doing something dangerous, or indirectly – by not doing something they should have) then they may be fined or prosecuted. So it's really important that you get to grips with all the key health and safety issues in your organization.

Organizational guidelines

Each organization has its own specific safety issues. In some it could be chemicals, in another it could be dangerous machinery or electricity, and in others it can be computer use.

As well as meeting the requirements of all the health and safety laws, your organization should have its own systems relevant to the kind of workplaces in which employees do their jobs. Employees should be trained where necessary, and they should also be informed about new developments or changes which affect their health and safety. Managers should make sure that everyone in their team is clear about health and safety issues, and that they follow any relevant procedures.

Don't miss any training sessions provided by your employer. It really could make a life or death difference to you or a colleague.

Common sense

A lot of health and safety is just common sense, wherever you are – at work, at home or elsewhere. It's things like:

- not leaving boxes or other objects lying around in corridors – people can trip up them
- not letting wires, cables or packing string trail or dangle – people can trip over or get caught up in them
- never mixing electricity and water

- not trying to do DIY when you've got no specialist knowledge – get an expert to do the job
- not causing fire hazards – with matches, cigarettes, lighters, blow torches, heaters, radiators, cookers, etc.
- always using any protective equipment you're given for your job – hard hat, ear defenders, goggles, safety shoes, overalls, gloves, etc.
- never using any chemical or chemical-based products in small rooms or cupboards where there isn't any fresh air
- not using computer keyboards for long periods of time without regular short breaks (ten minutes per hour) away from the screen, preferably standing up
- adjusting any screens or monitors so the top is level with your eyes
- making sure your chair is at the right height so you don't sit badly
- making sure any equipment you use is safe, well maintained and in the right position to prevent muscle strain and glare
- not lifting or moving heavy weights or awkward loads
- taking care not to spread or catch infections and diseases
- taking proper breaks and holidays.

First aid

Every workplace should have people who have passed a first aid course and are prepared to handle any first aid needed. The number of first aiders needed depends on the size and type of your organization and on its main activity. Sometimes they will need some specialist training (if your organization deals with anything particularly dangerous – such as chemicals, mining, hot liquids or metal, etc.) and they should have regular update sessions.

There should always be someone nearby who can deal with people involved in an accident. Mostly they only have to sort out minor cuts and bruises, but occasionally they will have to cover until a doctor or ambulance arrives.

It there isn't a first aid expert around and you're on the spot, remember these rules:

- get help immediately (colleague or ambulance)
- speak calmly to the person who's had an accident even if you think they can't hear you

- if it is a possible sprain or break – don't move them or any bit of them (arm, leg, finger – *never* their head, neck or back)
- check for breathing, and if necessary, loosen belts and collars; if it's safe to move them put them on their side with their knees bent and check their mouth is clear
- cuts and bleeding – try not to make contact with their blood (use gloves, plastic bags or a cloth if you can) – wrap something around a bad cut or press something on to it to stop the bleeding (shirt, towel, blanket)
- electric shock – *never* touch the person affected directly or with anything metal or wet until you've turned off the electricity supply (plug or mains)
- heart attack or not breathing – they need expert help immediately – don't try to do anything unless you've been trained
- above all, don't panic.

Other health, safety and fitness issues

Access

Organizations are having to look at making their workplaces and any customer outlets accessible to people with various disabilities. For example, wheelchair users and people with limited mobility need:

- wide corridors and aisles with level floors (no ragged carpet tiles or ripped lino)
- wide doorways with doors that are easy to open and that don't spring closed
- ramps rather than steps.

People with limited vision and blind people need:

- obstacle-free corridors and rooms
- clearly-marked doors (large letter or braille text signs)
- well-lit stairs and rooms (for those with partial sight).

People with impaired hearing and deaf people need:

- flashing lights as well as telephone bells and alarm bells
- clear signs (as they will read rather than hear information).

The great thing about these kinds of improvements is that they make workplaces safer places for everyone – brighter and easier to move around with clearer information available.

Smoking

Smoking is a hot topic in the UK! Some people insist on their right to work in a smoke-free environment. While some smokers agree that it can be anti-social to smoke at work, others feel they should be free to smoke. The health risks of smoking are known, and a few employers have completely banned smoking in the workplace. (In some cases, because of the safety hazards, and in others, because of the health hazards.) Some organizations have specific smoking areas (for employees and customers) and allow workers to take reasonable breaks. Very few organizations still allow people to smoke when and where they like. Make sure you know and understand the rules on smoking in your organization.

Alcohol

Alcohol is another tricky issue at work. Again, some organizations in the UK have banned drinking completely – usually for safety reasons (where people have to operate machinery or drive, for example) – both in the workplace and for people on duty but off-site (so you can't go for a drink in your lunch break and then return to try to do a job needing concentration, accuracy and a steady hand). However, other employers have a flexible approach, knowing that employees will drink socially with customers and colleagues, during and after work. In this kind of organization it's up to you to act responsibly – if you know that even half a pint of shandy slows you down and makes you behave like an idiot then *don't drink* during working hours.

It's generally best to leave alcohol for after work. Remember that it may be fun to get pissed after work with your colleagues – or at the office party – but you have to go back to work the next day. If you behave badly off-duty, word will get around. Enjoy yourself, but not so you can't remember why and how. And try to leave work at work. Avoid gossiping, arguing or spreading rumours about colleagues over a drink – you could lose friends and cause problems for yourself at work. This applies particularly in organizations which still allow (or even encourage) regular drinking – in and outside the workplace. Don't fall into the bad habit of drinking too much (tempting though it may be, especially if it's free), being too loud, getting offensive and having regular hangovers. Nobody wants to work with someone who's always in need of a drink.

Drugs

Drugs and work don't mix. Drugs are generally a bad idea (unless medically prescribed – most are illegal and addictive), and there are many better ways to spend your time and money. Employers see drug users as a major health and safety risk, and some test potential employees for drugs use (even for what you might see as leisure use) before offering jobs. If you want to get and keep a job, don't do drugs.

Safe sex

Many people go out with others they meet at or through work. After all, you spend a large part of your life there. As far as sex and work go, there are three main rules:

● never have sex at work (no matter how daring or funny an idea it might seem)
● never discuss a colleague's sexual performance with others at work
● never tease, embarrass or chase someone – to get them to go out with or sleep with you, or after they've gone out with or slept with you (this is sexual harassment).

And whoever you're having sex with, always have safe sex.

Health and fitness

No, this isn't a joke! It helps to be fit if you want to be able to cope with work and life. Most employers will ask about your medical history when you apply for jobs, and many ask new recruits to have medical examinations. This is partly to check whether employees are likely to develop any serious conditions or even die (which can be really expensive for employers with medical schemes or life insurance) and partly to help employees check on whether they should be making any changes to improve their health.

Some organizations offer advice on health issues and others even provide cut-price fitness club memberships. Most small employers don't, however, so it's usually up to you to get to grips with your own exercise and diet.

Exercise

Don't turn the page! You might not think exercise has anything to do with work – but it's important to keep fit and healthy if you want to survive long hours, boring days or stressful times. Here are a few hints:

- try to move around your workplace as much as possible – take the stairs not the lift if you can, go over to people's desks nearby rather than phoning them
- if you have a sports hobby or leisure activity, keep it going in the evenings or on your days off
- if you don't currently do any sports, try out several and take part regularly. Remember there are seasonal ones (football, tennis) and ones you can do more easily all year round (badminton, swimming). And if all else fails, get a personal trainer (sharing them with someone else cuts the cost)
- join a club at work if you can – some organizations have competitions and leagues which can be fun and introduce you to people from other teams
- exercise often makes you feel better.

Eating healthily

Sometimes, work gets so busy that it's difficult to eat properly, or at all. Remember that you'll work better if you eat sensibly and regularly (cars run on petrol, not air) and drink plenty of liquids (especially if there's air conditioning and in hot weather). Try to avoid lots of snacking. Crisps are handy but not good to eat three times a day, chocolate's great but not for breakfast! The general guidelines are:

- cut down on fatty and sugary foods
- eat plenty of carbohydrates (pasta, rice, bread, potatoes)
- have at least five portions of fruit and vegetables a day
- eat several smaller meals each day rather than one large meal, and avoid big meals anyway (especially at lunch) unless you have a very physical job that burns off a lot of energy
- drink plenty of water and other non-alcoholic drinks.

Try not to eat while you're working – take a break. If there's a canteen at work, check whether it does the kind of food you want to eat (and check out the prices – it might be subsidized). If not, put in a suggestion! If that doesn't work, find a good sandwich shop locally or bring in your own. Make sure you eat a range of different things and don't have the same meals all the time (at work and at home) just because it's easy or quick. Cost can be a problem, but 'healthy' food can be as cheap – if not cheaper – than snack foods, over-processed stuff and ready meals.

Working environment
Many of us spend a lot of our time working, often in a particular place – an office, a shop, a factory or a vehicle. Sometimes it can feel like being locked away – not being able to move about or get enough fresh air, feeling bored with the same old routines. Your work surroundings have a lot to do with how you feel at work and how effectively you work. It's widely agreed that horrible work surroundings can make people feel fed up so they slow down and switch off. But a bright, pleasant, safe work environment can help people to feel positive, motivated and cared for. Your employer should be prepared to invest a bit of time and money in your work surroundings (a coat of paint, some new furniture, better lighting, knocking down a wall or putting up a partition, etc.) but there are also a few things you can do to improve where you work such as:

- keeping your work area tidy. It really helps if you get rid of messy cups, chuck or recycle piles of old paper, clear out any useless furniture or machinery, and keep clutter off the floor (one of the most important items in any work area is a large bin). Clear your work surface and work area every day before you go home (this is often a health and safety requirement)
- asking if you can use some of your team budget for a few plants, or a kettle, or some cheerful mugs, etc. If there's really no spare money at all, then you could suggest clubbing together and putting in some cash each
- cheering up the staff room or rest room. Posters and postcards are great, adding a bit of colour to a dull wall (but make sure they aren't offensive – sexist, racist or generally rude)

- involving colleagues in improving their work area – get a bit of team spirit going, so everyone will feel it's worth making an effort to brighten things up
- above all, taking responsibility for keeping the workplace tidy and as pleasant as possible.

Point to remember
Health and safety is your responsibility as much as anyone else's. Not taking care and following guidelines can mean you put others at risk as well as yourself.

Representing and involving employees

Many employers in the UK used to get along by 'hiring and firing' people when it suited them. They weren't interested in employees' views on work or employees' rights at work. But some employers realised that employees are more likely to feel part of an organization – and to work well and enthusiastically – if they feel they have a real say in decisions affecting their jobs. These employers involved employee representatives through works councils or staff associations and they were sometimes prepared to work with ('recognize') relevant trade unions too. Today, there are many ways of involving employees at all levels in an organization, helping employers make better quality decisions which employees then feel they 'own' too.

Trade unions

There are currently 74 official trade unions in the UK making up the Trades Union Congress. Around 6.6 million UK employees are in a union (about 30% of the workforce). While unions started over 100 years ago to protect workers in traditional 'blue collar' (non-office and trade) industries, many union members are now in 'white collar' (office and professional) sectors. A lot of the people in flexible and insecure jobs don't join unions – either because they don't know about them, or because they can't afford the subscription, or because they don't feel it would help them in any way.

Trade unions got a fairly bad name in the 1970s for causing

strikes and being unco-operative when dealing with employers. They lost some of their power due to various laws in the 1980s, and many unions have since developed good working relationships with employers at national, regional and local levels.

If your organization 'recognizes' one or several unions, you should get details on how to join when you start work. It usually costs between £5 and £10 a month. There are often a few colleagues who act as union representatives – a role they have on top of their job for which they're allowed reasonable time off. You may have different groups for the union members in your organization depending on people's jobs – or different unions involved. For example:

Training organization		Factory making food	
Union	MSF (Manufacturing Science and Finance)	**Unions**	TGWU (Transport and General Workers Union) for most production workers, AEEU (Engineers and Electricians Union) for technical employees
Union groups	– Administrators – Trainers – Managers		

There are three main roles for unions – consultation, negotiation and representation.

Your union representatives will arrange meetings for each group – regularly or when needed – to discuss various issues. They then feed people's views back to managers, usually at joint consultation meetings where union and management representatives discuss issues affecting employees and the organization. An agenda should be circulated in advance so that union representatives can consult their members in order to put across their views at consultation meetings. Consultation sessions may also be arranged when there's a major business issue – such as redundancy, relocation or a buy-out.

Union representatives also represent their members in negotiations, which normally happen once a year to decide any increase in pay or changes to benefits. The union representatives clearly want to get the best possible deal for their members and the management negotiators want to keep within budget, so it can be a long and frustrating process.

A union representative can also provide support to any individual member or group of members who face a difficult situation – such as discipline, harassment or redundancy. This is the union representative's specific representation role.

If things get out of hand in any of these three areas, the union representative can call in an official from the union, and they can also get advice on employment law and other issues from the union when they need it.

If there's no 'recognized' union where you work, you can still join a union and be an individual member, able to contact the experts at the union if you need support or advice.

Your organization may also have a staff association which handles consultation, negotiation and representation for employees (but isn't an official TUC union).

Works councils and staff councils

Some UK organizations want to involve employees but not necessarily through a union. They may set up a works or staff council where elected employee representatives meet management representatives to discuss business issues.

Works councils can be very effective (and there are European Union guidelines on how they should work), but they focus on consultation and tend not to get involved in the same kinds of negotiation or representation as unions.

Getting involved

It can be really worthwhile to represent your colleagues – as a union or staff association representative or on a works council. But it can also be hard work on top of your job and take up a lot of time and energy – even if you are allowed some time off from your job. However, you do learn a lot about communication, consultation and negotiation – how to make a case, how to put across colleagues' views, how to see both sides of an issue, and how to find common ground between what you think is fair and what management is prepared to offer. You have to remember two main things:

- you're representing other people not your own views. It's not an opportunity to have a go on issues that bug you – and you may have to put forward views with which you don't agree
- you have to be able to balance two roles – doing your job and being an employee representative – and sometimes you'll have different priorities for each one.

There are many ways of getting involved in consultation and decision-making without becoming an official employee representative. You could offer to represent your team on a project (to discuss if and when to relocate, or to look at job changes, for example). You could send in feedback on a proposal sent round by managers (asking for comments on changing the pay and benefits package, or suggesting major changes to departments, for example). In these sorts of situations, always remember the ABC communication rules – appropriate, brief and clear, focusing on *what* not *who*. Never use consultation as an excuse to have a go at somebody, as you won't be taken seriously and you may cause trouble.

Finally, your manager should regularly involve you in decisions about your job and your team's activities, and they should ask for your views on major decisions affecting the whole organization. It's part of a manager's role to keep you informed, to consult you and to feed your views back up.

Point to remember
Getting involved in things outside your job can be a great learning experience and can help you develop new skills and get additional experience. But make sure you can keep what you do in your job separate from what you do as an employee representative.

Part Four

Ways of working

Ways of working

Very few people can work on their own, without having to fit in with other people. Even people who work on their own at home have to link up with other people at various times.

Sometimes work doesn't feel much like a team effort. Like on days when you seem to have all the boring tasks to do and everyone else seems to be doing something more interesting and enjoyable. And sometimes it might not be clear who your team is. Some managers say things like *'we're all in this together, team'* or worse *'we're all one big happy family'*. The truth is, you probably fit into several teams – your immediate team (the people you work closely with most or all of the time); your unit or department team (who you work with towards the same targets); a specialist or one-off team (for a project, for example); your organizational team (other bits of the organization linked to your unit or department); and the whole organization itself, which should be working as a big team. Of course, in smaller organizations it will be easier to feel part of various teams because you're likely to come into contact with most other people there. But in an organization with thousands of employees your immediate team and even your unit/department team can feel like a very small part of things. So your immediate and next level team is important to you – to give you a sense of identity (who you are and how you fit in) and purpose (why you're bothering and why it matters).

Successful teams

In order for teams to be successful, every team member needs to play their part. You can't be an effective team if half of you don't care. So it's partly your team leader or manager's role to give every team member a sense of:

- purpose – what they're there to do and why
- pride – in themselves and their team (why it's good to be part of it)
- personality – what makes their team special.

It's also part of the manager's role to sort out any:

- problems – particularly people not working well together
- practicalities – resource, location, money or time issues
- personality clashes – people not getting on (which is usually upsetting and disruptive).

Working in a team

It's up to team members to take responsibility for being a team member and working effectively with colleagues. To do this you need to:

- understand your own job – its purpose and priorities, how to do it and what you need to do it
- other people's jobs – not every detail, but roughly what they do and how they do it
- where and when you overlap – what you need from them and what they need from you
- the skills they use to do their jobs.

Many people work brilliantly on their own but are useless team members because they don't know what anyone else does, they don't understand how their job fits into everyone else's, and they never tell anyone what's going on in their job. Sometimes it's just because they haven't thought about the team, or nobody's ever explained how the team should work, or they just aren't good at communicating. Occasionally, it's because they don't want to be part of a team, or they've decided they don't like or trust their team members, or they want to keep their work secret so they get any credit themselves.

Most organizations can't work like this – they need high-performing and flexible teams where everyone's working towards the same goals. But people who aren't good at teamwork have often had bad experiences in the past – perhaps being bullied by previous colleagues, or having credit taken by another colleague for their work – so they need to be given confidence in their new team. It's a manager's role to work with any team members who find it hard to fit in, but other team members can help. For example, you can take the time to explain your job to colleagues in a friendly way and to learn about their role.

Good team members need:

- good communication and listening skills
- an understanding of other people's priorities
- the ability to work as part of several teams at any one time
- confidence in themselves and their ability to contribute to the team.

If you feel you're having problems as a team member then try and think about *what* the problem is (as ever, don't focus on *who* you're having problems with but *what's* not going right between them and you) and decide whether there's anything you can do about it. If they're getting cross because you're missing deadlines, then meet your deadlines. If you think it's something you can't deal with, then talk to your manager. If it's your manager you're having a problem with, then talk to a responsible colleague – the HR manager, or your employee or union representative.

Point to remember
Team working is one of the key skills organizations look for when they promote or recruit people. It's worth trying to improve the way you work with other people.

Flexible working

Lots of organizations see 'flexibility' as one of the answers to all their problems. Production problems, problems with competitors, loss of customers, customer demand, staffing problems – you name it, flexibility's the answer. And it's true that organizations can no longer survive by running themselves in an inflexible, old-fashioned way. They need to be flexible in two main ways:

- flexible *ways* of working – teams being creative and motivated, looking for new ways of meeting targets, keeping costs down, delivering a more effective service to colleagues and customers, coming up with bright ideas
- flexible working *time* – people working non-standard hours in order to make the organization as effective as possible.

Flexibility is great in theory – but a major problem is that some employers want it all their own way. They expect employees to be flexible in how and when they work, but they aren't flexible in return. So flexibility needs to be a two-way deal with benefits for the organization and the individual.

Flexible ways of working

This book covers most of the skills and knowledge you'll need to be a flexible team member, such as communicating well, taking responsibility for tasks and projects, managing your time, having good basic skills and developing new skills. But your manager needs to make sure that you and your colleagues still have clear objectives and a chance to do your job. Being flexible shouldn't mean constant chaos! It may occasionally mean a big team effort or a change of routine, which should be discussed at team meetings, your regular 1:1 meetings and annual appraisal (see Part Three). It may also mean responding to customers' needs more quickly than usual (whether they're 'internal customers' – colleagues – who need your help, or external customers who are buying your products or using your services).

Increasing flexibility usually involves shorter timescales – it's no longer any good to say you'll get it done when you can (think about what you expect when you order or buy something) and you have to juggle deadlines and priorities all the time. So you need to be flexible in the way you manage your workload and work with others.

Another aspect of flexible working is a flexible working location, such as:

● teleworking (working away from the organization's main locations)
● homeworking (if you work from home, make sure you keep your work separate from your home life as far as possible)
● mobile working (travelling around from place to place)
● 'hot desking' (moving around within the office using whatever space is available).

Employers benefit from flexible working by having the people they need doing the right thing in the right place at the right time – as cost-effectively as possible. Employees can also benefit by being able to work when it most suits them, so they can balance their work with other priorities. However, you and your manager should always discuss any move towards flexible working – to make sure that it meets both your needs as far as possible.

If your manager suggests that you move from full-time standard working to some more flexible way of working, you need to ask questions, think about what it will mean for you and – if possible – agree a way forward which will suit you both.

Sometimes organizations make groups of people change the way they work (moving from full-time to part-time, for example) and give them hardly any choice. This is not a good idea, as it leaves a bad feeling, good people may leave and it may be illegal. It's also unfair on people who really need the earnings from a full-time job.

If you feel you need to work more flexibly (perhaps to look after someone, or to do some part-time study to update your skills) then you need to find out what options your organization offers. There should be a list in your employee handbook or personnel procedures, or you can ask the HR manager or your employee/union representative.

When flexible working isn't the 'norm' (as shift work and part-time working may be, for example) some managers are not keen to encourage it. This is usually because they may be put off by having to manage someone who works differently (it makes communication with a team difficult if some of them are around at different times, for example), and they may think people who 'can't be bothered' to work full-time standard hours are lazy and not committed to the organization. They may also be jealous that other people seem to have a life outside work.

So you need to think through what would work for you and be prepared to meet the organization half way in order to match flexible working to the needs of you and your employer. And remember, it's not only difficult for a manager whose team members work in a variety of different ways, it can also be difficult for employees to cope with changes in the way they work, and the effect it has on their lives and income.

Point to remember
Look for flexible ways of working and flexible working patterns that free you to do a good job and have a balanced life too. But don't expect flexibility to be the answer to all your problems.

Balancing work and life

All work and no play doesn't just make you a dull person, it's also very unhealthy and unnecessary. We all have times when we need to work flat out (doing extra hours or overtime) to finish a project, meet a deadline, complete a customer order or even earn some extra cash. But this should be your choice, and the exception not the rule.

You are more effective at work if you're able to spend 'quality' time doing other things out of work (hobbies, sport, time with friends and family, volunteering, nothing). It is also better if people feel able to bring their whole self to work – so they don't have to pretend that they're not a parent, or that they're not passionate about a hobby. We should all behave appropriately and focus on our jobs while we're working and being paid, but it's stressful to have to put on a completely different personality just for work. For example, you don't stop being responsible for your children when you're at work.

Good employers will have flexible working practices and provide options to enable people to balance their work and home lives. These may include:

● part-time work
● job-sharing
● term-time working
● home working
● emergency leave
● career breaks
● childcare advice and support
● flexible training and development opportunities
● information in newsletters, on notice boards, etc.
● senior-level role models (particularly men who work part-time)
● links with helpful specialist organizations and networks (see p. 179).

The important thing is to get some balance into your life. Work will occasionally spill over into home life (you'll talk about it, bring work home or work extra hours) and personal life will occasionally spill over into work (you'll worry about it, and have to take time off). But overall, you need to set boundaries in your life so one part doesn't overtake another, while accepting that everyone has to juggle lots of different priorities (even if it doesn't look as if they do – they're either good at getting the balance right, or they're hiding their problems and difficulties).

If you're feeling that you haven't got the balance between work and life right, try asking yourself these questions:

1 Am I having a bad day or week?
2 Have things been difficult for a while?
3 Are things getting worse?

If you answered 'yes' to question 1, it probably means there's a temporary problem – like a sudden extra workload or the children being on half-term. These things happen, sometimes you can plan for them, sometimes you can't. It's helpful to think about ways of managing this kind of problem if (or when) it happens again.

If you answered 'yes' to question 2, there's probably something you need to tackle to get some balance back into your life again. Try and work out where you think the main problem is (always too much work, regular childcare problems) and take some action. If you can't take action, at least get some advice. Try your manager, HR manager, employee assistance helpline (if your organization has one), or even a good friend who will understand and be able to see things from a different angle. They might come up with ideas for tackling things.

If you answered 'yes' to question 3, you need to *sort things out now*. It isn't good for you, your family and friends, your colleagues or your organization when you can't balance your work and your life – and when the situation is getting worse. You need to talk to your manager, your HR manager or one of the specialist advice services listed on p. 179. It may be that you're trying to do too much, or that you need some help either at work or at home – or both. Don't carry on feeling pressurized, stressed or even ill. There's no need – and it could cause more problems in the long term.

Research among 5,500 UK managers (by the business magazine *Management Today* and the consultancy WfD) showed that many people are struggling to balance their work and home lives. These are their 'top ten' lists of problems and solutions:

Problems

1 missing children growing up
2 putting work before home and family
3 moving home for their employer
4 missing leisure/hobby time
5 travelling from home, short-term
6 breaking up with a partner
7 travelling from home, long-term
8 missing out on work-related education
9 not having or postponing children
10 not being able to form relationships.

Solutions

1 work fewer hours
2 change the organizational culture
3 work flexible hours
4 reduce or avoid commuting

5 work from home
6 change jobs or consider relocating
7 have more staff
8 earn more
9 retire
10 reduce stress.

Taking control of your life is easy to suggest and not nearly so easy to do. But it's worth asking yourself these kinds of questions:

- Am I managing my time and workload as effectively as I can? (see p. 54)
- What are my main priorities for the next three years?
- How much money do I need to earn?
- What do I want to achieve and learn – at work and in the rest of my life?
- How much time do I put aside for *me* and the things I want to do each week?

Thinking about these kinds of issues may help you to get a better balance between work and home. For example, you may decide that your job and income are top priorities for you – in which case, you need to come to terms with the fact that the rest of your life may need to take a back seat for the next two or three years (this may mean less clubbing, or dropping one of your hobbies, or sorting out some childcare). On the other hand, you may decide that your priority is to spend as much time as possible learning a new skill or studying, or looking after your children, or taking a break to travel – in which case you have to do some serious thinking about how you cut back on the time you spend working – at least for a few months or years – and this will mean changes to your income and career.

Point to remember
Most people cope brilliantly with too much on their plates at various times in their lives, but you shouldn't have to cope all the time. If things get too much, you may end up feeling stressed. Sort it out now.

Part Five

Problem areas

Problem areas

Stress

We all use the 'stress' word a lot – *'I'm stressed out', 'I'm under a lot of stress at work at the moment', 'I'm finding my job very stressful'* and so on. It's certainly a feature of most people's lives, but what exactly is 'stress', what causes it, and why do some people seem to be so much better at dealing with it than others?

Stress is, basically, feeling out of control. If you don't tackle it, your performance, self-confidence and health can all suffer. It isn't that feeling of excitement or anxiety you get occasionally, when you face a big challenge and your heartbeat speeds up. That's a positive thing, as it helps you concentrate, focus and perform to the best of your ability. Negative stress is, however, when you have too much on your plate – too much to do and not enough time, resources or skills to do everything. It can be too many of the things you can't cope with on top of all the things you can cope with. Or a sudden change in your circumstances which means you can't cope with things you could manage before. Sometimes, people get stressed by one relatively small extra thing. Other people only notice their stress levels rising if lots of things happen or change.

Why stress occurs

So stress is a *personal* thing. It's important for you to work out what puts *you* under pressure and how *you* handle it. The trick is to get to grips with stress issues as early as possible (to stop them becoming problems) and to stop yourself developing the stress habit. Getting hooked into a stress cycle is a bad idea and ruins your life at and outside work.

Here are the three factors involved in causing stress.

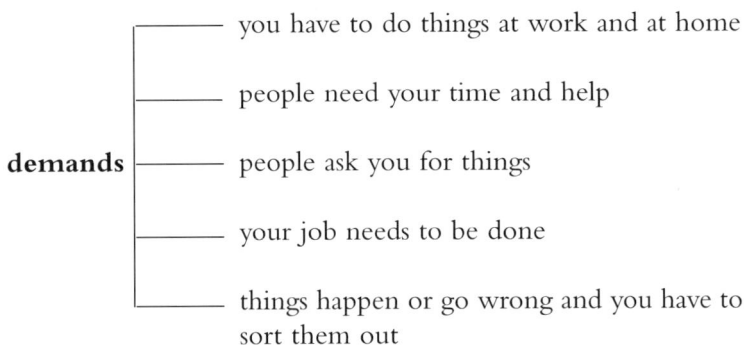

demands
- you have to do things at work and at home
- people need your time and help
- people ask you for things
- your job needs to be done
- things happen or go wrong and you have to sort them out

The above list is what life looks like – a series of demands on you at work and at home. For example, one week you might have to visit your friend in hospital, pick up your brother from the airport, sort out and pay your household bills, get the boiler mended – all on top of doing your job, and you might also be having a bad week at work!

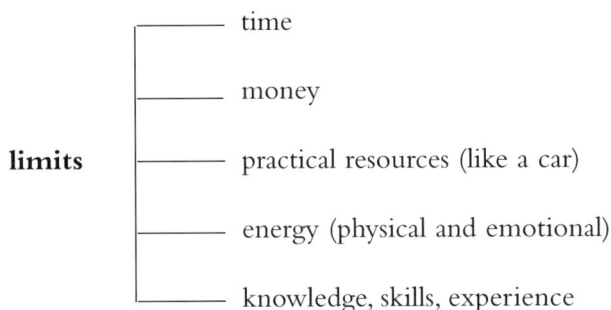

limits
- time
- money
- practical resources (like a car)
- energy (physical and emotional)
- knowledge, skills, experience

The above list is the reality of life – we don't always have enough time or resources to do our job in the hours available, let alone cope with all the other things we need to do. You may have money problems (short-term or longer-term). You may not have some of the practical things you need which make life a bit easier. You may be feeling run down or have a cold, or be having relationship difficulties. And you may be expected to do things at work which you don't feel capable of.

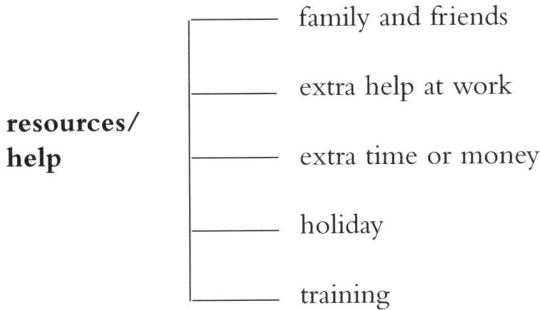

resources/ help
- family and friends
- extra help at work
- extra time or money
- holiday
- training

Sometimes (as shown above), help is available – and, if we're lucky, at the right time. You may be able to get family or friends to sort things out (be there for the boiler repairs, pick the children up from school, meet your brother at the airport, do the shopping). You may get some extra help at work – temporary or permanent – or be able to share your workload with someone else. You may be able to take some time off work to catch up and relax, or you could be lucky enough to get some extra cash (year-end interest on your account, for example) so you can pay someone to sort something out for you. You could be due a holiday when you can sleep properly, eat properly, and spend some time on the things you haven't been able to sort out – as well as going away and having a complete break, of course. And you could go on a training course which gives you the extra skills and confidence to deal with your job.

So stress isn't *what's happening* to you – it's about whether you can *cope with the amount of things* in your life. Dealing with stress is about keeping some balance, being realistic, and being fair on yourself – and others. You don't have to be Wonderwoman or Superman. If there are too many demands on you, too many limits, and not enough help and resources – then you may feel stressed.

Signs of stress

These are some of the signs to look out for in yourself and others.

Behaviour

- short-tempered and irritable
- upset and angry
- saying things you don't mean
- crying
- mood swings and changes in behaviour.

Health and fitness

- slowing down or hyperactive
- tired or can't sleep/sleep too much
- eat more or less
- overweight/underweight
- headaches
- other aches and pains (muscles, stomach, joints)
- indigestion
- panic attacks
- spots or bad skin.

Emotions

- feel lonely and unloved
- mood swings
- feel people are out to get you
- don't believe in yourself.

Managing stress

A lot of people think that because stress is about being on overload, then coping with stress is about taking time off or getting away from all the things that make you feel stressed. That's not true. What you actually need to do is to sort out all the things you're dealing with into three lists:

- things you *can't do anything about*
- things you *can stop doing*
- things you *can do something about*.

So your lists might look something like this:

- *can't change*
  big project at work with short deadline
  parent's new partner
- *can stop*
  saying 'yes' to everyone at work
  nagging partner
- *can change*
  car breaking down
  rows with best friend
  messy flat
  workload management.

Accept that there are things you *can't do anything about*: the big project is your responsibility and part of your job; you may not like your parent's new partner, but it's their choice and you just have to accept it.

Then look at the things you *can stop doing:* don't nag your partner when you feel stressed – it doesn't solve anything and it's causing more problems; don't say 'yes' to everything people ask you to take on at work – say 'no' and give a reason (see p. 35 on assertiveness) or suggest when you could help and schedule it in (see p. 54 on time management).

Finally, set yourself some targets for the things you *can do differently*: get the car fixed, use public transport, or budget to buy a new car.

Don't take your stress out on your best friend – look at how you're communicating and the signals you're giving (see p. 32 on interpersonal skills), and talk things through with them (*'I'm sorry I've been so snappy recently. I don't mean to get at you. I've been feeling really stressed, and I'm afraid I took it out on you because I knew I could rely on you to put up with it! I'm trying to sort my life out now – have you got ideas on how I could . . . ?'*).

Set aside some time (a couple of hours, an afternoon) to sort out your flat, pay your bills, hoover, catch up on your washing. Maybe invite a friend round, play some music and make it time off, not just chores you hate doing. Then, make sure you spend one hour a week keeping things tidy. And finally, look at why you're always so overloaded with work (apart from not being able to say 'no'). Are you doing the key things first or leaving them until last, and are you wasting time doing unimportant things first? Are you managing your time effectively?

So here are the stress management guidelines.

- Get real – you can't do everything.
- Get to know what makes you feel stressed and how to recognize when you're feeling stressed.
- At the first signs of stress, take an hour to list all the things you have to do under the three headings (can't change, can stop, can change).
- Plan your time, always leaving a bit spare each week for yourself.
- Focus on the key bits of your job (don't get distracted) and the other important things in your life.
- When things get too much at work, talk to someone outside the organization – colleagues can mean well but they can make things worse. Everyone needs a network of supporters who each give a different view (sensible, flattering, good listener, honest feedback, etc.).
- Get to grips with *why* you're overloaded and feeling out of control (don't just make lists of *what*), and take action to stop things piling up again.
- Always do something to take your mind off things for at least half an hour each day – read a magazine, newspaper or book, watch TV or play a computer game, watch a film, take some exercise, play music.
- Look after yourself, eat well and keep fit. Treat yourself occasionally to things you enjoy.
- If you feel you can't cope and can't sort things out for yourself, get help and advice – don't battle on. Try an HR colleague, your manager, a friend or family member, or a counsellor.

Point to remember
Manage your stress levels – at work and outside work – so stress doesn't take over your life.

Handling difficult situations

It often seems as though *people* are the problem at work. But if you want to tackle any problems you face, you need to look at *what* is wrong, not *who* is wrong. Here are the kinds of problems you might come up against, followed on p. 141 by some guidelines on tackling difficult situations.

Difficult situations

The manager from hell

Yes, we all have at least one! But it's not funny, it's usually irritating – and it can even make you fed up or depressed. You need to work out what the real problem is, as you can't do your job well if you're worried about your manager.

The customer from hell

The saying goes 'the customer is always right', which means that you have to do everything you can to meet their needs or deal with their complaint. However, you do not have to put up with a customer being abusive or offensive. Being bullied or harassed isn't part of your job description.

The colleague or team member from hell

Nobody gets on with everyone they have to deal with at work or in life. It's only natural that you will get on fine with some people and not so well with others. But we all have to try and work together to get the job done, even if our colleagues are never going to become our best friends. Try not to focus on personalities. Don't get into the habit of thinking *'I hate Mel'* or *'I don't like Asubi'*, but work out what's bugging you. For example *'It makes me feel uncomfortable when Mel sits too close to me or puts her hand on my knee'* – the issue here is about personal space and possibly sexual harassment. Or *'I feel angry when Asubi always disagrees with me in team meetings'*. The issue here is the disagreement which embarrasses you (see p. 35 on how to be assertive and raise difficult issues with people).

Lack of support and advice

Sometimes you might feel as though you're last in the queue for everything. Everyone else seems to be getting praise, advice and guidance from their manager, but you just seem to have to carry on alone, no matter how many times you ask for help.

This can be because your manager or team leader is simply short of time, and you always seem to choose a bad time to ask for help. Or it could be that they don't think you need help – that you're capable enough to cope on your own, or that you need to learn by trying out your own ideas and maybe learning from a few mistakes. It could also be a form of bullying – making you feel uncomfortable for some reason. Or you might not be asking in the right way. Complaining and whinging isn't a good start – and are you getting your request for help across clearly enough (saying exactly what the problem is – lack of resources, lack of knowledge, etc.)?

Lack of training and development opportunities
Another case of feeling last in the queue. It may be that you feel other people are always offered training and development opportunities first, or that your requests are always refused, or that your manager never asks you about your training and development needs.

This can be because you're not being clear about what you feel you want to do – so your message isn't getting across. Or it could be that your manager doesn't feel they can spare you for several days' training at the moment, or that they think you're skilled enough already.

Of course, it could also be a form of discrimination against you or favouritism towards others – or your manager may be scared you'll move on if you get too good at your job.

Verbal or written bullying
This is when you're regularly teased, insulted, critized or threatened – face to face or by memos, e-mails, or even graffiti. It could be because you're new, because you're different from the others in some way (younger, different sex or race, etc.), or just because you're the easiest person for a bully to pick on. Or you could have started it, by something you said or did which made someone else feel uncomfortable or threatened – so they're trying to get their own back. Bullying's really about power, not about wanting to push someone around or be nasty to them.

Physical bullying

This is pushing people around or getting violent towards them. It can be service-users or customers who bully or are violent, not just colleagues. A few organizations still have embarrassing or dangerous 'initiation rites' – that is, things done to new people to 'make them part of the team'. Physical bullying is unpleasant and can make your working life miserable. Remember, bullying's a power thing, so victims are usually making someone feel threatened in some way.

Sexual harassment

This is unwelcome or uninvited behaviour due to your sex which makes you feel uncomfortable or threatened. It can be verbal or physical, and it can be from someone of the opposite sex or the same sex. It can be embarrassing, irritating, frightening or violent behaviour. Sexual harassment's about power – someone feels threatened by you and they want to get back at you (for example, you may be in line for a promotion which they feel they should get) so they behave badly towards you and harass you using sex as the hook.

Racial harassment

This is unwelcome or uninvited behaviour on the grounds of your racial or ethnic background – which makes you feel uncomfortable or threatened. It can be verbal or physical, and it makes you feel embarrassed, irritated, frightened or in danger.

Remember that racial harassment's about power. Someone who feels threatened may use a victim's race as the hook for bad behaviour and harassment.

Constant criticism

This can involve regular, sarcastic comments, lack of praise or acknowledgement, or regularly being put through the disciplinary procedure. Sometimes it's face to face criticism but it can also be to or though other people (behind your back) or on paper – copied to you or not seen by you (even though you often find out about it).

Sometimes you may be causing the problem, and if that's the case you need to work out why you aren't coping with your job or getting on with your colleagues. But it may also be unjustified criticism, with your manager or colleagues always seeing the downside of things regarding you. In this case, criticism can make you feel fed up or depressed – which is not fair and doesn't help you do your job well.

Discrimination

Discrimination means being treated less fairly than other people due to a certain factor – your age, sex, race, religion, background or any disability, for example. You can be discriminated against in terms of selection for jobs, training opportunities, pay and benefits, promotion, discipline, dismissal or redundancy. But you need to be clear that it is discrimination (a decision based on *who you are*, not *what you can do*) and not a reasonable decision based on how you do your job or whether you can do a job. Some forms of discrimination may be illegal (sex, race, pay, disability).

Regularly missing out on promotion opportunities

Sometimes you go for one job after another and never get promoted. It can be really upsetting and make you lose confidence. Unfortunately, it can be due to prejudice or discrimination (people's views about you, based on their values and experience, not on what you are actually capable of). But sometimes it might be that you're going for the wrong type of job, or that you need to focus on getting some training or experience before you try to move on.

Something dishonest or dangerous is going on at work

If you know about something dishonest or dangerous which is being kept secret in your organization (like fraud or pollution) you may need to 'blow the whistle' – that is, tell someone outside – to prevent a major crisis or disaster. There may be some legal protection for 'whistleblowers'.

Health problems

Some people battle on despite being really depressed or unwell. This makes thing worse for them and may put others at risk. They need to get help and support as early as possible.

Family problems

People are sometimes afraid to own up to having family problems in case it looks as though they can't manage their lives. Some organizations discourage employees from 'bringing their personal lives to work' and you certainly need boundaries, but people need to be able to sort out serious family problems (someone being seriously ill, or a death) – often with no notice – without feeling guilty.

Stress

If someone's behaviour changes when they are under pressure, they may be suffering from the negative effects of stress. The situation needs to be tackled as early as possible, for everyone's sake (see p. 134).

Money worries

Not being able to pay bills is a big worry for most of us at times. Some people may even resort to fraud or theft in desperate circumstances. They should always get help as early as possible (see p. 67).

Tackling difficult situations

The key thing about handling problems and sensitive issues at work is to *tackle the issue* not to focus on or attack others involved. One important thing is to look at whether your behaviour is contributing to the problem – or even causing it in the first place – and whether you're communicating effectively and getting your message across.

It's best to try and sort things out between you and the other person/people involved wherever possible, as that often means you work better together from then on. Use your 1:1 meetings with your manager, or book a meeting with another colleague, and make sure you communicate clearly, listen properly and be assertive (not aggressive or passive). But if you've done what you can to improve the situation and things are still as bad, then you need to:

● Get advice and help from someone else in the organization – an HR person, another manager (perhaps more senior), an employee representative or trade union official. They may recommend that you follow an appropriate procedure, such as grievance. The grievance procedure sets out the steps to go through if you want to make a formal complaint. You need to write down your complaint and find out who to send it to. You should then get a formal reply explaining what's being done to investigate your complaint. Usually, if your complaint is looked at and rejected, you can appeal – and your complaint then gets looked at by someone at a more senior level (and can go on to further stages too).

Sometimes you'll be asked to attend a meeting to explain your side of things. The person you have a problem with might be there too. It's a good idea to take a union representative or colleague with you – and always make notes of what was said and agreed.

Remember that you're trying to get a decision which sorts out your problem and meets the organization's needs. So listen to all the suggestions and offers made regarding your complaint, be reasonable, and try and sort things out.

If their help doesn't solve the problem, you might need to:

● Get advice and help from someone outside the organization – in the UK this could be a full-time trade union official, someone from the Citizen's Advice Bureau, an advisor from a specialist organization or a lawyer.
● Resign and leave, although you should try to have something to go on to.
● Consider taking your case to an employment tribunal if you feel you've been unfairly treated.

Point to remember
Everyone has problems at work, but don't let any problems affecting you get out of hand. Tackle them before they get too serious, and always get help and advice if you feel you can't cope.

Part Six

Moving on

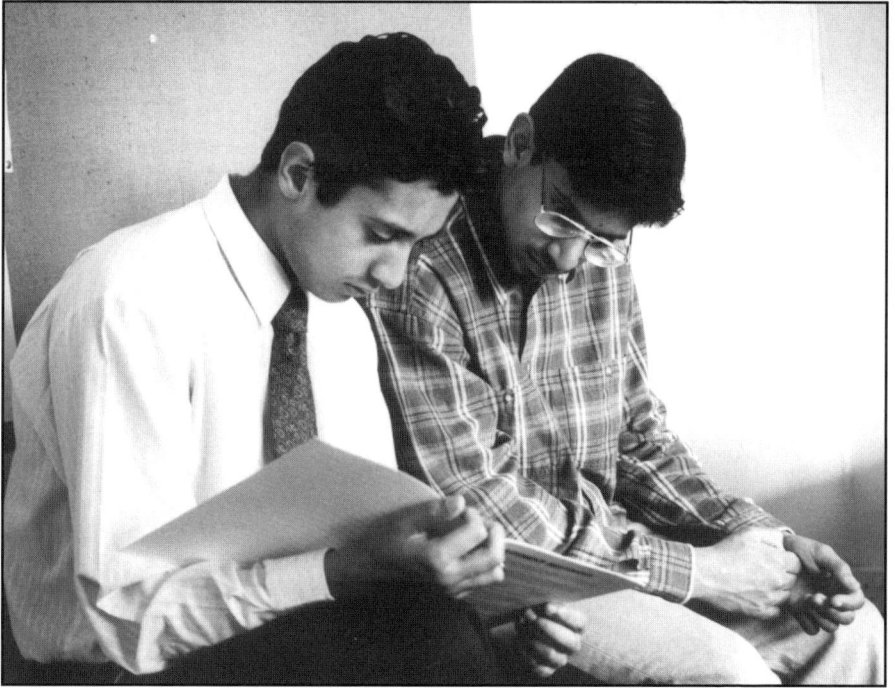

Moving on

You can never get enough training and learning opportunities. Work is changing so quickly these days that you need to keep updating your skills and knowledge in order to keep up. Also it's fun to learn new things, in as many different ways as possible.

Training is mainly about teaching people what to do, and how and when to do it. You can be shown by a colleague, or you can go on a training course. Organizations have lots of basic things they need everyone to be able to do – like using the phone, the word processor or computer – as well as the right skills and information for your particular job. Training is usually focused on what people or teams *need* to know and do. In some cases you don't have to understand a lot (like how the whole computer system works) but you need to know enough for your job.

Learning is broader, more about *how* you work things out rather than *what* you're taught. So you sometimes learn about new things for the sake of it – or without having a specific purpose – because it adds to your overall knowledge and ability to perform well at work. You probably learn quite a lot without knowing you've done it – picking things up from your colleagues, manager, customers, friends. You can learn from problems and difficult situations as much as from positive development opportunities.

You learn a lot informally, just when you're doing everyday things, and you don't have to be in a formal learning situation (like going on a course). So learning is more than training, although training is part of learning.

An example is that you can go on a training course to practise and improve your communication skills, but you will continue learning how to use them over time and building on what you were trained to do on the course.

Skills development is what it says – adding to and building on your skills. This helps you cope with new things and do things more quickly, easily and effectively. You probably have skills you don't know you've got – and you probably think you have skills which you don't really have. Many managers, for example, think they have good communication skills but, in fact, they can't get a clear message across – in person or on paper. But they're probably very good at something else – project management, for example, although they might never realize it.

Always keep a record of your training, learning and skills development activities. If your organization doesn't give you a training file or log book then start your own. Remember that you don't learn just through your job but also through other things you do outside work. It all counts.

Employers look for qualifications and work experience when they recruit, but more and more organizations are focusing on people's skills and what they've learnt. This is because jobs aren't as easy to pin down as they used to be – you may have to be very flexible as part of a team, or you may change jobs regularly as the organization moves on. So organizations aren't just looking for someone who can do a certain job any more – they want someone who can use their skills in a flexible way. That means you need to:

- keep a record of your training, learning and skills
- take advantage of every training and development opportunity you get
- think about your experience in terms of skills not jobs
- focus on learning across the whole of your life – it doesn't stop after school or work.

Here's an example of a job description (also used in Part Three) showing the skills and experience the job holder would need to have:

Job: team administrator
Key activities:

- handling post, phone calls, e-mail and diaries for three team consultants
- word processing consultants' paperwork (letters, memos, etc.)
- attending consultants' meetings with clients to provide administrative input
- project managing consultants' projects
- acting as contact point for other teams and departments.

Additional activities:

- contributing to other teams' projects where appropriate
- briefing consultants on technology updates (word processors, telephones, etc.)
- organising team 'away days'.

Skills and experience needed:

- time management
- project planning and management
- written communication
- typing and proof-reading documents
- building relationships with colleagues and customers
- understanding and using technology.

Sometimes organizations use the word 'competencies' when talking about skills. It's a way of saying 'things people can do', and it is used to explain what skills people need in order to do their job effectively.

Your organization should give you some priorities for training, learning and skills development – usually linked to your job, your team's needs and what the organization needs. Employers try to make the best use of the resources (time and money) they put into development by planning and reviewing, like this:

But there also needs to be a balance between what the organization gets back from your development and how you benefit (you're more likely to learn if you're interested).

If your organization or manager doesn't set you any development targets then you need to plan and manage your own development and find as many ways as possible of learning new things. Achieving your performance targets will often depend on developing your skills, and some of your targets should be about learning and development.

Finally, if you're worried about finding the money for training and development, there may be various loans and grants you could consider, including (in the UK) a Career Development Loan or the new Individual Learning Account. Contact your local Employment Service or the Learning Direct helpline (see p. 179 for more details).

Point to remember
The world of work keeps moving on, and so should you. Keep updating your skills and take advantage of any training and learning opportunities – at work and outside work.

Self development

Everyone learns new things all the time at work (even when they don't realize they're doing it!). Gradually, people become more capable of doing various bits of their jobs through learning 'tricks of the trade', finding shortcuts to getting good results, and working out how to get things right first time. People usually outgrow their jobs after a while, and move on when and if they can.

Today there are few if any 'jobs for life', so it's important not only to develop your skills and experience as much as possible but also to plan what you want to learn next. Some development opportunities come along by chance – but you need to organize others. You'd be amazed at how many different ways there are of developing your skills and experience to improve your chances of moving on in the world of work. Here are some suggestions:

1   Read relevant books or magazines.
2   Listen to cassette tapes 'on the move'.
3   Do computer-based learning (at work or home) using CD ROMs, etc.
4   Study for a qualification.
5   Visit and learn about other organizations.
6   Join a project team.
7   Do some outdoors training.
8   Attend a training course.
9   Go on secondment to another team or organization.
10 Do a 'job swap' with someone.
11 'Workshadow' someone (follow them around to learn what they do).
12 Stand in for someone when they're on leave.
13 Take on new job responsibilities.
14 Serve as a union or employee representative or a health and safety representative.
15 Take part in a community project out of work hours (youth club, environment project).
16 Find a mentor or a coach.
17 Write a report.
18 Take part in a debate or make a presentation.
19 Join a professional networking organization.
20 Do an evening class.

There's no competition to see who can clock up the highest number of self development activities, but it's important to be as broad-minded as possible. Don't just go for the easy (or cheap) opportunities, like training offered by your organization to help you do your job better. It's best to try and mix something more challenging (perhaps outside work) with the standard opportunities at work – and that kind of broad, self-motivated learning gives a positive message to future managers and employers. Here's the kind of checklist you could use for the three main areas – skills development, learning and personal development.

Area	Target/Deadline
Skills development What do I need to learn or get better at for my job?	
When will I see a real difference?	
Learning What subject do I want to learn about or learn something new about?	
By when will I have learnt something new (read a book, watched a TV series, participated in a project group, etc.)?	
Personal development What do I want to feel more confident about as a person?	
How could I make this change?	
When will I sit down and review how I'm doing?	

There's no point in having targets if you ignore them or you don't check to see how well you're doing and how much progress you're making! You need targets to be **SMART**, that is:

S – **Specific**   – don't be vague

M – **Measurable**   – you need to know whether you're making progress and when you've got there

A – **Achievable**   – don't be too ambitious, otherwise you'll feel a failure

R – **Realistic**   – make sure you can find ways of moving towards your target

T – **Timed**   – put a deadline on your targets.

List your targets and keep a record of them in your learning logbook. For example:

Target	By when
go on time management course	February 1999
attend evening classes – holiday French	Mid-1999
join project team	September 1999

Remember that you should write down every single piece of self development in your learning logbook. This is a record of what you learn during your life.

It's amazing how quickly you can forget all the valuable things you've learnt and done, so it's worth getting yourself a ringbinder file and some pages which you can fill in as you go along. A page in your learning logbook might look like this:

What achieved	When achieved	S = skills L = learning P = personal
attended 1 day time management course	September 1999	S
was member of disability awareness project team	October 1998 to June 1999	L/S
went to evening classes – holiday French	January to June 1999	P/L
attended a half day course on new PC package	August 1999	S
started volunteering once a week at local youth group	July 1999 onwards	P
watched series about European business – sent off for factsheet	Spring 1999	L

Point to remember
You are responsible for planning and managing your own development. Make sure you set yourself targets and record what you do and learn.

Coaches and mentors

Many successful people have 'coaches' and/or 'mentors'. If you're lucky, your manager may be great – giving you a clear idea of what's expected of you and guidance on how to do things; your colleagues may be supportive and helpful; and your friends may be sympathetic and give you loads of good advice. If (like most of us) you're not so lucky, your manager may be OK (good at some things, not so good at others), you may get on with a couple of colleagues and you may occasionally get some sense out of your friends. So it's helpful to have someone else either to help you develop your skills (a coach) or to act as a sounding board and role model (a mentor). A mentor can also be a coach, but good coaches don't necessarily make ideal mentors – as a mentor's role is quite broad and takes a special mix of skills.

What a coach does

A coach at work is much the same as a sports coach, focusing on enabling people to perform really well and have maximum confidence in themselves. You may not be keen on any particular sport, but you've probably watched some of the finals on TV – tennis, football, basketball, swimming, rugby, athletics. You'll know how the top sports people look – focused, committed, confident, able to find that extra effort when needed – and often they win. Coaching is more about giving people the confidence to keep learning and improving than just about teaching people what to do (it's not how to hit the ball, it's about believing you can hit a winning shot). Coaching at work is about giving someone the confidence to learn and develop new skills, not about teaching or training them what to do. So a coach doesn't need to be an expert in your line of work, but they do need to understand what you do and to be very good at motivating and advising you, based on their experience and their belief in you.

You'll probably find a coach by accident – by working with someone in a project team, for example – and realize that they can give you the confidence and support you need to get on in your job. They're usually someone in your organization. If you get on well, why not ask them whether they'd be prepared to make a bit of time to work with you – as your coach? Some people are flattered and get enthusiastic about this kind of suggestion, particularly if they've done it before. Others may be scared, because they don't think of themselves as being able to help others. Either way, you could suggest an initial session to see if it works – maybe half an hour one lunchtime. Explain that you think you could both learn useful things – your coach could develop their coaching skills and you could develop new skills and confidence. For any coaching session, set the following agenda, using **GROW** as a reminder, as in the example below:

G – **Goal of session:** look at why I keep missing deadlines

R – **Reality of situation:** identify exactly what happens and why

O – **Options for action:** list all the possible things I can do about the problem

W – **What and when:** agree what I'll try first, and for how long/by when.

At your next session you need to go over what has changed, explain how you feel about the progress, and set new targets for action using **GROW.**

Your coach at work can be your manager, another manager or a colleague with the right experience. It's great if you find a good coach, and it can make a real difference to your confidence and performance.

What a mentor does

A mentor may coach you, but they have a broader role including:

- helping you plan and manage your career
- encouraging you to take responsibility for yourself, your work and your life
- offering support and encouragement
- helping you learn and develop skills, knowledge and experience.

A mentor may at different times act as a:

- coach (see above)
- role model – giving you an example to follow and learn from
- networker and 'door opener' – providing you with contacts and opportunities to help you achieve your goals
- counsellor – listening to you and helping you work out solutions to problems, even telling you (perhaps unwelcome) home truths
- sounding board – giving you a chance to test ideas.

Mentors don't get involved – they should keep some distance (unlike a friend) so they can handle any of the five roles when necessary. You need regular contact with your mentor (it's best to plan times to talk over the phone or meet in the early stages) but as time goes on you may get in touch when you need to, not according to a timetable. Your mentor doesn't have to work in the same organization or even the same field (in fact, it's often better if they don't) but they need to agree to be a mentor and to have the following:

- enough time
- good communication and listening skills
- a confidential approach
- the confidence to question and challenge
- experience of work and life
- the enthusiasm to support and take an interest in you
- your trust.

Often, good mentors have had good mentors themselves and they want to return the favour. It can be very rewarding to be a mentor – for relatively little time (say, half an hour a fortnight, or an hour every six weeks) you can see someone develop in confidence and skills and make progress in their job and life. You'll probably become friendly with your mentor – as you have to be open with each other – but it's best not to become close friends, as it can be difficult to separate mentoring from socializing! However, people who end a mentoring relationship after an appropriate time often stay friends. Other people stay in touch with their mentor for a long time, even though they both move on in their lives.

So why do you need a coach or a mentor at all? Well, maybe you don't, if you get enough support, advice and feedback anyway. But work can be tough at times for all of us – it's hard to make progress, hard to move on – so a good coach or mentor can make all the difference.

Point to remember
A coach or mentor can make a positive contribution, supporting you as you develop skills, experience and confidence.

Your next job

Just as there are lots of ways to develop your skills and experience, there are different ways of moving on to a new role or job. Relatively few people now stay long-term in the same job, mainly because organizations and the jobs within them are changing quickly. (Some organizations seem to be almost permanently restructuring, reorganizing or changing their culture). There are also fewer clearer career paths, so people tend to do a broader mix of jobs across their working lives – and some people have several different jobs at the same time (such as two part-time jobs, or several contracts as a freelance worker or consultant).

Moving on

You need to make a success of your current job, but you also need to think about where you'll go next. Here are some of the options:

Secondment or job swap

You go and work somewhere else (in the same or another organization) – sometimes swapping jobs with someone else. Secondments are usually for a fixed length of time, and then you either go back to your job or move on to a new opportunity. Secondments are a good way of getting more experience and making new contacts.

Promotion

You often have to apply and be interviewed for vacant jobs in your organization – and, if you're lucky, you get offered a new job. (It can be unfair for jobs just to be offered to people, as it doesn't give others a chance). Don't always look for a more senior role or more pay. Promotion doesn't have to be upwards – it can be sideways, giving you the chance to develop new skills and get wider experience (and lots of organizations are now 'flatter' – so there's less chance of an upward move anyway). Only go for jobs you're keen to do, and certainly don't go for a job just because it's got a more important job title or pay.

End of placement

You may have to move on at the end of a work placement or work experience scheme (for example, after six months' employment in the UK under the New Deal programme). If you've shown you're keen and you've developed your skills, your employer may offer you a more permanent job (in the case of a sandwich course, when you've finished your studies). If not, you need to plan your next step.

Redundancy

Occasionally, your employer will not need people to do certain jobs any more. Sometimes it's to cut costs, or at other times it's because the organization is changing the way it works. The important thing to remember is that it's the *job* that is redundant, not the person in it. If your job is made redundant it doesn't mean you're useless or on the scrap-heap. You need to take any help offered (careers advice, etc.) and make sure you get any redundancy payments due to you.

Resignation

If you apply for and get a job with another employer you have to resign from your current job by handing in your notice. (Never hand in your notice unless you are sure about what you're moving to – either you have written confirmation of the new job offer or you have decided to take a break from work for some reason). Most UK employers expect a standard amount of notice (a week, a month, three months or whatever's in your terms and conditions) but many are flexible and will agree a leaving date that suits you and them. They can insist on a minimum of a week if you've been working a month or more (ERA 1996 s.86).

First steps

So, when you're planning to move on or have to move on, what do you need to do? Most people put together a 'CV' (curriculum vitae) – a list of things you've done in your life. Another approach (which covers the same ground) is to put together two main summary sheets covering your:

● education and career
● skills and experience.

The education and career summary should list your:

- secondary school(s) and college(s), including exam results
- job(s) and employer(s), including the main responsibilities in each job.

Your most recent job should be at the top, and the least recent item (probably secondary school) should be at the bottom. The skills and experience summary should list as wide a range of skills as possible, grouped under relevant headings and put in the most appropriate order for each job you apply for. Headings might include: communication and interpersonal skills, project management, customer care, sales, administration – whatever's right for the job.

If you use only these two sheets when applying for a job you also have to send a covering letter with clear details of your address, contact number and why you think you're right for the job.

Applying for jobs

Often you'll see a job advert and decide to apply. Occasionally someone will let you know about a job vacancy. Either way, you need to be ready for the application process. This can involve any or all of the following:

- getting an application form and job details
- filling in an application form and/or sending a CV
- preparing a covering letter and additional information
- going for an interview (with one person or a panel of people)
- going for a second interview
- attending an assessment day (to do tests, group exercises or have additional interviews)
- being made an offer (make sure it's in writing)
- negotiating pay and benefits
- providing the names of people who can give a reference about you
- having a medical check-up
- agreeing a date for starting work.

You may, of course, be told that you didn't get the job (after interviews and tests) or that they don't want to see you for even a first interview. In that case:

- be polite (you may apply to them again)
- try and get some feedback if you can (you might learn something helpful)
- look at your paperwork (is there anything you could improve next time?)
- stay positive (everyone gets turned down for jobs)
- try again (it might be worth talking to friends or anyone else who might be able to give you some useful advice or ideas).

Remember, application forms should be completed neatly and clearly, and any extra bits of paper should be relevant and easy to read. And always make sure things are returned by the deadline.

On your application you should not have to put personal details (apart from your name, address and contact number) which are not relevant to your ability to do the job (like how old you are or whether you're male or female). Unfortunately, many UK organizations still ask for these details on their application forms. However, employers also ask for a whole range of additional details on a separate or detachable form, usually called something like a monitoring form or an equal opportunities form. These forms are confidential and don't stay attached to your application – so they shouldn't affect any recruitment decision about you. Instead, they help an organization to check that a good mixture of people are applying for jobs. For example, these monitoring forms may ask for:

- age
- sex
- ethnic background (options often look like this):
  - white
  - British black
  - black Caribbean
  - black African
  - black other
  - British Asian
  - Indian
  - Pakistani
  - Bangladeshi
  - Chinese
  - Other Asian

- whether you're married, single, living with someone
- whether you have children
- whether you have any of the following types of disability or medical conditions:
  - physical or mobility impairment (can't move around very well or quickly)
  - sensory impairment (limited or no sight or hearing)
  - learning disability
  - mental health needs
  - chest diseases and heart conditions
  - conditions such as diabetes and epilepsy, allergies, symptomatic HIV or an AIDS-related illness.

Interviews

To make a good impression in interviews:

- Prepare – think about the job, why you're a good candidate, and what will make them remember you instead of the other applicants.
- Wear tidy, appropriate clothes and clean shoes.
- Be positive – even if you're nervous, keep focused on what you want to say.
- Listen carefully – answer the questions they ask, not the ones you want to answer!
- Use positive communication and interpersonal skills – avoid jargon, be clear and brief, look at the interviewer and don't be aggressive or passive (even if they get tough with you).
- Think about pay and benefits beforehand, but don't talk about money unless they raise it with you.
- Have a couple of questions to ask – look interested in the job and keen to get it.

It's impossible to give much more advice on handling interviews as each one is different. Above all, you need to use positive communication skills, explain your skills and experience clearly, and sell yourself well.

Life planning

What about if you're not planning to move on just yet, but you know you will in a year or two? You need to have long-term goals and aims, and to give yourself a sense of direction – and you can do something about that now. It's easy just to keep going in your job (and your life) until one day you realize you're bored and need a new challenge. Don't let that creep up on you.

You need to write out a life plan, and then review and update it every year. Alongside your performance targets this gives you a set of goals for work and life – and you can record any learning achievements in your learning logbook (see p. 151).

Here's how to put your **life plan** together:

- think about the next year, the next three to five years, and the next ten years (three different timescales)
- think about your work priorities and your personal priorities
- dare to dream! This is about what you really want to do and be
- don't think about *how*, think about *what*. Put down what you'd really like to do and be, even if you can't see how to get there.

Your life plan might look like this:

Date of this lifeplan	*next year*	*3-5 years*	*10 years*
Work	get new job in sales	move into marketing start part-time diploma course	run own PR business
Life	do scuba-diving course start local youth club	find long-term partner go swimming with dolphins	have family and move to country

It's amazing how writing down your aims like this can focus the mind, and help you make other decisions in life (which training course to go on, when to move house, etc.). And you will change your priorities as time goes on. The first week of a new year is a good time to have an annual look at your plan (preferably not straight after a party!) or when you're on holiday and have a bit of breathing space and a sense of perspective.

Finally, remember that a good coach can help improve your self-confidence, and a mentor can act as a role model and give you good feedback. They can often help you turn dreams into plans, and plans into reality.

Point to remember
It always helps to have a sense of direction and something to aim at – even if you change your goals over time.

Part Seven

Useful information

Useful information

Employment law

There are laws and regulations to protect people at work. Some of them are very effective, but others don't stop bad practice by some employers and managers. It helps to have an idea of the key laws affecting employees (UK regulations are listed below). But they're long and complicated and it would take a whole book to summarize them. So remember, you should be able to go to your manager, your HR contact, or your union or employee representative if you're worried about anything. You shouldn't try to be your own lawyer.

Key employment laws
(numbered where listed in text)

1	Employment Protection (Consolidation) Act	1978
2	Employment Protection Act	1975
3	Employment Act	1980
4	Employment Act	1982
5	Employment Act	1988
6	Employment Act	1989
7	Employment Act	1990

8	Sex Discrimination Act	1975,1986
9	Race Relations Act	1976
10	Disability Discrimination Act	1995
11	Social Security Act	1986
12	Trade Union Act	1984
13	Trade Union and Labour Relations Act	1974,1976
	Trade Union Labour Relations (Consolidation) Act	1992
14	Transfer of Undertakings (Protection of Employees Regulations)	1981
15	Wages Act	1986
	Equal Pay Act	1970
	Fair Employment (Northern Ireland) Act	1976,1989
	Fair Employment Monitoring Regulations (Northern Ireland)	1989
	Contracts of Employment and Redundancy Payment Act (Northern Ireland)	1965
	Rehabilitation of Offenders Act	1974
	Rehabilitation of Offenders Exemptions Order	1975
	Rehabilitation of Offenders (Northern Ireland) Order	1978
	Rehabilitation of Offenders Exceptions Order	1979
	Trade Union Reform and Employment Rights Act	1993
	Data Protection Act	1984
	Sex Discrimination (Northern Ireland) Order and Amendment	1984

Statutes and other enactments are written in legal language and jargon, so most people have to get help not only on legal issues but even on understanding what the law is in the first place. If you want more details, ask your manager, contact your HR officer, get in touch with your union officer or visit your local library or Citizen's Advice Bureau.

However, it's helpful to know about five particular terms relating to the law:

● *Statutory* – laid down by government (comes from 'statute' which is another word for an Act of Parliament). Every employee has statutory employment rights, as explained in this Part of the book.

- *Contractual* – in your employment contract. In practice all employees have contractual rights and benefits beyond their basic statutory rights.
- *Individual rights* – what each employee is entitled to.
- *Collective rights* – what groups of employees are entitled to.
- *Legislation* – another word for Acts of Parliament, etc.

Employment contract

When you join an organization you should be asked to sign a contract and you should get a copy to keep. Don't agree to start work with an organization without seeing, reading, understanding and signing a contract.

Do not agree to anything in the contract that sounds odd or unfair. Ask them to explain it and send you a letter confirming what it means in writing. Always ask to see your 'terms and conditions' of employment. In some organizations, this may be the contract, and in others there may be extra paperwork.

If the organization wants to change your 'terms and conditions' of employment (the way in which you're employed, the hours you do, the job you do, etc.) they must first get your agreement and send you a formal letter explaining the changes. Your employer cannot make substantial changes to the way you're employed without your agreement.

Keep all the formal letters you get from your employer – your copy of the contract, details about your pay, confirmation of any changes in the way you're employed plus (very important) all your pay slips. They may look boring or confusing to you, but they show lots of details which your tax office may need, and they can be useful if you have to give proof of your earnings at any time (if you want a mortgage, for example).

You don't have to keep them forever but you must keep them for at least three years for tax purposes, and it's best to keep them for five if possible (if you've got the space).

Laws about the individual and work

Dismissal

Most employees with at least two years' continuous service get statutory protection against unfair dismissal. A fair dismissal can be for:

- lack of ability (or relevant qualifications)
- bad or dangerous behaviour
- redundancy
- not following the law or other regulations
- any other major justifiable reason.

Employers must follow appropriate procedures when disciplining someone, before it even gets to dismissal. They should:

- give the person an informal and verbal warning first
- go through the disciplinary procedure, giving the person the chance to improve performance or behaviour
- make sure senior managers are involved
- let the person bring a representative with them (union or colleague)
- make sure all sides are heard (there might be reasons why the person's performance has been a problem) before deciding on any action
- make sure people understand any penalties – why they are to be imposed and what they mean
- give the person a chance to appeal
- not dismiss anyone for a 'first offence' unless it's for something really serious (theft or violence, etc.).

Employers may have to pay compensation or re-employ someone if they're found to have unfairly dismissed them.

Laws: 1,4,7,8,14
Time off

Employers must allow employees reasonable unpaid time off for public duties (e.g. school governor). The following employees are entitled to paid time off:

- pregnant women for ante-natal appointments
- trade union officials to carry out their duties and undergo relevant training
- elected representatives to undertake their duties

- pension scheme trustees to undertake their duties
- safety representatives to perform their duties and relevant training
- redundant employees with two years' continuous service, reasonable time off to seek alternative work or training.

Laws: 1,3
Wages/pay
Employers can't take money out of people's pay unless it's:

- required by law (tax, National Insurance, social welfare, etc.)
- agreed by the employee in advance
- in the employee's employment contract.

Similarly, an employee can't change any payments they owe their employer without written agreement or legal reasons. However, an employer can take money back if:

- someone's been overpaid in error
- the employee's been involved in industrial action
- there's a written agreement
- there's a legal decision.

If employees' working hours are cut or if they can't go to work for some reason (like workplace health and safety hazards), those who've been there for at least one month get 'guarantee' pay – a minimum payment calculated according to legal guidelines or employer rules (whichever's better). However, employees won't get guarantee pay if they've not been available for work or have refused certain types of work.

If an employer goes out of business, employees who lose their jobs are entitled to various payments (such as statutory redundancy pay from the state – see below).

Laws: 1,3,4,6,15
Notice periods
Giving notice means confirming a change in employment. So if you resign, you have to 'hand in your notice' or 'give notice' that you wish to leave. Employees have to give at least one week's notice after they've been there a month (and there may be a longer timescale in their contract). An employer also has to give notice when making employees redundant.

Employees legally are entitled to the following minimum notice from their employer:

- one week after at least a month's continuous employment
- one week for each year's continuous employment of 2-12 years
- 12 weeks after 12 or more years' continuous employment.

These timescales may be longer in some organizations' contracts. Employees get full payment for the notice period, even if there's no work for them to do, or if they're sick.

Laws: 1
Maternity
Pregnant women get:

- paid time off for ante-natal care
- protection from dismissal related to pregnancy
- statutory maternity pay for 18 weeks (if employed for at least 26 weeks)
- return to work after maternity leave or − if there's no job available − redundancy pay.

Length of maternity leave entitlement depends on the employee's service:

- 14 weeks basic leave for all employees with less than two years' service by the 11th week before the expected week of childbirth
- 29 weeks leave following the actual week of childbirth for those with two years or more service by the 11th week
- Statutory maternity pay is payable for 18 weeks maximum to employees with 26 weeks service by the 15th week before expected week of childbirth.

Some employers pay contractual maternity pay which is more generous than SMP and give longer periods of maternity leave even though they are not statutorily obliged to do so.

Laws: 1,3,11 (including statutory maternity pay regulations)
statutory redundancy pay
Generally, full-time employees with at least two years' service get a lump sum payment from their employer, depending on their age and length of service. The statutory minimum for each continuous year of employment is:

Age 18-21 years	0.5 week's pay
Age 22-40 years	1 week's pay
Age 41-64 years	1.5 week's pay

For statutory redundancy pay there is also a maximum weekly amount fixed by the government, and 20 years is the maximum time with an employer that can be taken into account. Employers have to give employees a written explanation of how redundancy pay is calculated.

Employees can lose their redundancy pay if their employer offers them their old job back or a suitable alternative job and they refuse to take it. They can try the replacement job for up to 4 weeks (or longer if it's agreed in writing that they need re-training) and still get the redundancy pay if things don't work out.

Employees don't have to work out their full notice, if they put in a request to leave earlier in writing and the employer agrees.

An employee who is made redundant is entitled to notice (or pay in lieu) in addition to statutory redundancy pay.

Laws: 1, 6, 7
Tribunals
Someone who feels they've been unfairly dismissed generally needs to complain to a tribunal within three months of leaving the organization. A tribunal is a type of employment court which involves both sides (the employer and the ex-employee) – often with representatives. There are three members – a lawyer plus two people from business and industry who have a good understanding of employment law. The tribunal can decide that:

● the person should be taken back by their employer
● a compensation sum should be paid based on certain guidelines (depending on the dismissal circumstances).

Tribunals were originally meant to be quite informal. Over the years (they started in the 1960s) they have become increasingly informal. The government is therefore now arranging for ACAS to set up a less formal voluntary arbitration service as an alternative, but whether this is successful or not won't be known for some time.

Laws: 1, 2, 3, 4
Union membership
Employees normally have the right to be a member of an independent trade union which isn't controlled by an employer, and they also have the right not to be forced to join an independent trade union.

Employees are allowed reasonable time off for union activities – as representatives and as members.

Secret votes (ballots) are required by law in certain circumstances, and on other occasions employers must allow secret votes when requested by the union.

Laws: 1, 2, 3, 4, 5, 6, 7, 12, 13
Written information employers must supply
Employees must get a written statement confirming the date they started their job and stating their employer's name and their own name. This must arrive within 13 weeks of starting work. It should also include:

- job title
- rate of pay – or, if it varies, how it's calculated – and when it's paid
- hours of work (plus a note of any extra time that has to be worked)
- number of days' holiday, holiday pay, sick pay, any details about absence due to sickness, pensions
- notice periods – what employee and employer must give
- details of the discipline and grievance procedures or say where there is an explanation – (staff handbook, etc.)
- who you can go to with a grievance or to appeal against a disciplinary decision
- clarification of the type of pension scheme if appropriate.

You also should get regular pay statements which explain all amounts (and, in the case of redundancy, a statement explaining how redundancy pay is calculated). If you have at least two years' continuous service, you can also ask for written details of any dismissal (redundancy following discipline, etc.) and should get it within 14 days of your request.

Laws: 1, 6
Change of ownership
If an employer's business is sold or transferred to another organization, employees may also be transferred. They can only be made redundant for specific business reasons – in which case the usual redundancy guidelines apply.

Laws: 14
Part-timers
Part-time employees are entitled to the same statutory rights as full-timers. When the EC Part-time Workers Directive comes into force in the UK in April 2000, part-timers will also be entitled to the same contractual rights as full-timers (e.g. rates of pay and fringe benefits).

Laws about groups of individuals at work
Collective bargaining, negotiation and consultation
Trade unions have the right to:

- be consulted about redundancies, mergers and business transfers
- be given information relevant to collective bargaining
- have officials who are given paid time off for union activities
- appoint health and safety representatives.

Trade unions and employers often draw up and sign collective agreements which set out all the issues on which they will consult together. This can include any of the following:

- employment terms and conditions
- working conditions
- recruitment, redundancy and job content
- how work is allocated among employees
- discipline, grievance and dismissal
- negotiation, consultation and representation
- industrial action.

A 'closed shop' is where one or several unions and one or more employers agree that employees must belong to a specific union. It's sometimes used to cut down the number of unions an employer deals with and some collective agreements are 'single union' agreements. 'Closed shops' are not technically illegal but in practice are seldom formed these days. This is because an individual who loses his job, or cannot get a job, because of a closed shop agreement will be entitled to enhanced compensation, a large part of which is likely to be payable by the union rather than the employer.

Laws: 2, 3, 4, 5, 6, 7, 13, 14
Releasing information
When asked, employers have to give union representatives any reasonable information relevant to collective bargaining (unless the information could harm the organization, an individual or the country). Information might be about redundancies, selling the business or job changes. It might include timescales, money details and business reasons.

When there are redundancies involved, employers must:

● consult unions (even if it's only one person whose job's at risk)
● let the Employment Department know if 20 or more redundancies are planned at the same location.

Laws: 2, 14
Industrial action, strikes, 'working to rule'
Unions have to hold a secret vote (ballot) and get the majority of members' agreement before industrial action. Disputes can be over any of the issues listed under 'collective bargaining'. Those involved have to be current employees likely to be affected by some issue under dispute.

'Picketing' (protesting at the workplace) is allowed if it is a peaceful way of putting a point across or getting others to stop work in support of the industrial action.

Trade unions are held responsible for the results of local action by their union members unless they send round written statements to say they don't support the industrial action.

Laws: 2, 3, 4, 5, 7, 12, 13
ACAS – The Advisory, Conciliation and Arbitration Service
This service was set up in 1974 and given legal authority in 1975. It's independent from the UK Government. Its overall role is to promote good industrial and employee relations by giving advice, publishing codes of practice, and helping to settle disputes between individual employees – to avoid them ending up at a tribunal if possible.

Jargon checklist

Terms in *italics, like this,* mean there's another bit of jargon to look at elsewhere

Appraisal: At school you had reports, at work you get appraisals. At the end of a given period your work is reviewed by your *line manager.* Appraisal is particularly important if your employer uses a *performance-related pay scheme.*

Benefits: Things you get on top of your pay (luncheon vouchers, subsidized meals, etc.).

Boss: Everyone has one. Don't forget that your boss probably has a boss too. It's worth trying to see things from your boss's point of view – so at least you can understand what's going on – even if you don't agree with them.

Business Process Re-engineering: BPR is supposed to be about the way your organization plans and works, but it's often about getting rid of a lot of employees and *rationalization.*

CC: Copy (it used to mean 'carbon copy').

Coach: Someone who gives you the confidence and skills to improve your performance.

Command and control: Strong downwards management (fairly old-fashioned) a bit like the army, where people have to follow orders and stick to rules.

Corporate: Another way of saying 'organizational'.

Culture change: Making your organization more open, effective and competitive (well, that's the theory).

Customer care: Putting customers first (including colleagues who are seen as 'internal customers').

Discrimination: Unfair barriers which prevent some people or groups from fulfilling their potential.

Diversity: Different types of people working in different ways (often linked to *equal opportunities*).

Downsizing: Term for making your organization smaller by making people redundant.

Early start: If you are good at getting up, an extra half hour in the office before others arrive can help you to stay on top of things when you start a job. Don't make a habit of it, though. (See *long hours.*)

Empowerment: The buzzword for trusting people to get on with their jobs, and take responsibility for decisions.

Equal opportunities: Removing barriers to access and opportunity faced by certain people or groups.

Expenses: Amounts you can claim back if you spent the money for a work reason.

Flip-chart: Large sheets of paper on a stand – people use felt tip pens for writing up notes on them in meetings and training sessions.

Freelance: Someone who works for themselves.

Harassment: Sexual, racial, verbal or physical harassment is a power thing and completely unacceptable. Get help and advice on sorting it out.

Human Resource Management: Used to be known as *Personnel.*

Just in time: Planning and managing stocks so you only have what you need, but you still meet every customer's needs.

Learning organization: Organizations that try to learn from their mistakes and improve all the time.

Lifelong learning: Keeping on learning in a variety of ways throughout your life.

Line manager: A technical word for your boss or manager. This is the person who is responsible for what you do (or not do) at work. Try and get on well with this person if you can.

Long hours culture: Where people feel they have to work long hours otherwise they're not showing enough commitment. The UK is said to have the longest average working hours in Europe. It's not a good thing and can cause *stress*.

Memo: A note circulated to colleagues – it should be clear and brief.

Mentor: Someone who acts as a role model, sounding board and guide.

Mission: An organization's goals and aims.

Performance-related pay or performance bonus: Some organizations think people work harder and better if they get bonuses for good performance – so they link their pay and performance.

Personnel: Often now called Human Resource Management – these people handle day to day employment matters (often including recruitment, pay, discipline, dismissal and sometimes also pay and pensions too).

Portfolio career: Mixture of jobs and types of job (freelance, full-time, part-time) – at the same time or during your working life.

Productivity: The amount of work done or things produced in the time available.

P45: The tax slip you get in the UK when you leave an employer.

P60: The annual tax slip you get in the UK showing what you've earned in the tax year and what you've paid in tax.

Quality: See *Total Quality Management* below.

Rationalization: Reorganizing or making people redundant.

Rightsizing: Making people redundant (like downsizing).

Right first time: Getting things right first time (linked to *Total Quality Management*) to save time and money.

Right to strike: There is no right to strike in UK law before taking a secret vote (ballot) for industrial action.

Seminar: Training session or course.

Strategy: An organization's plan for the next three to five years.

Stress: Feeling out of control.

Tactic: Short-term, planned action.

Teamworking: Doing your job while supporting others in your team doing their jobs.

Total Quality Management: Getting every part of the organization to work to high standards in how they work and what they produce or do.

Vision: What an organization aims at, long-term.

Whistleblowing: Telling the truth about something dangerous or dishonest in your organization – usually to an outsider.

Addresses and telephone numbers

Organization	Aim/role	Address	Telephone
Advisory, Conciliation and Arbitration Service (ACAS)	Provides help and advice on employee relations and employment law	Clifton House 83–117 Euston Road London NW1 2RB	0171 396 5100
Alcoholics Anonymous	Aims to solve the problem of alcohol abuse and help people recover from alcoholism	Stonebow House Stonebow York YO1 7NJ	01904 644 026
Basic Skills Agency	Provides advice and support on acquiring basic skills	Commonwealth House New Oxford Street London WC1A 1NU	0171 405 4017
British Dyslexia Association	Provides support and information to all those with dyslexia	98 London Road Reading Berkshire RG1 5AU	0118 966 8271
Carers National Association	Provides support and services, and campaigns on behalf of carers	22-25 Glasshouse Yard London EC1A 4JS	0345 573 369

Organization	Aim/role	Address	Telephone
Centrepoint	Aims to ensure that no young person is at risk because they do not have a safe place to stay	Bewlay House 2 Swallow Place London W1R 7AA	0171 544 5000
Childline	24 hour helpline providing a confidential counselling service to children and young people	Freepost 1111 London N1 0BR	0800 11 11
Citizen's Advice Bureau (CAB)	Provides free, confidential and impartial information and advice to everybody needing help	115-123 Pentonville Road, London N1 9LZ	0171 833 2181 check phone book for your local branch
Commission for Racial Equality (CRE)	Provides advice on employment and discrimination issues	10-12 Allington Street London SW1E 5EH	0171 828 7022
Community Service Volunteers (CSV)	Provides a wide variety of volunteering opportunities for people aged 16-35	237 Pentonville Road London N1 9NJ	0171 278 6601
Department of Social Security (DSS)	Provides free guides and leaflets on benefits	Richmond House 79 Whitehall London SW1A 2NS	0171 712 2171
DSS Pensions Information	Provides information on pensions	Freepost BS 5555/1 Bristol BS99 1BL	0345 313 233
Employers' Forum on Disability	Provides information and advice on employing people with disabilities	Nutmeg House 60 Gainsford Street London SE1 2NY	0171 403 3020
Equal Opportunities Commission (EOC)	Aims to eliminate discrimination and promote equality of opportunity between men and women	Overseas House, Quay Street, Manchester M3 3HN	0161 833 9244

Organization	Aim/role	Address	Telephone
Foyer Federation	Provides accommodation, training and job-search help	146-148 Clerkenwell Road London EC1R 5DP	0171 833 8616
Health and Safety Executive	Enforces the Health And Safety At Work Act 1974 and advises on health and safety at work	HSE Information Centre Broad Lane Sheffield S3 7HQ	0541 54 55 00
Institute of Personnel and Development	Provides resources and training on personnel and development issues	IPD House Camp Road London SW19 4UX	0181 971 9000
Learning Direct (DfEE)	Offers advice on a wide variety of learning opportunities	PO Box 900 Manchester M60 3LE	0800 100 900
Lesbian and Gay Employment Rights (LAGER)	Produces regular bulletins on lesbian and gay employment rights and issues, and can give advice to individuals facing discrimination at work	Unit 1G Leroy House 436 Essex Road London N1 3QP	0171 704 2205
ME Association	Provides advice and support to people affected by ME	4 Corringham Road Standford-le-Hope Essex SS17 0AH	01375 361 013
Narcotics Anonymous	Offers help to anyone who wants to stop using drugs	202 City Road London EC1V 2PH	0171 730 0009
New Ways to Work	Provides advice on flexible ways of working	309 Upper Street London N1 2TY	0171 226 4026
Parents at Work	Provides advice, support and services relating to working parents	Fifth Floor 45 Beech Street Barbican London EC2Y 8AD	0171 628 3565
Shelter	Provides services and campaigns for homeless people	43-47 Wellington Steet Sheffield S1 4HF	0800 446 441

Organization	Aim/role	Address	Telephone
The Samaritans	Volunteering organization for people who are despairing or suicidal	10 The Grove Slough SL1 1QP	0345 909 090
Trades Union Congress (TUC)	Provides advice and services relating to trade union issues	Congress House Great Russell Street London WC1B 3LS	0171 636 4030
Voluntary Service Overseas (VSO)	Organizes work placements abroad	317 Putney Bridge Road London SW15 2PN	0181 780 2266

Useful books

Allcock, Debra	Do Yourself a Favour	1993	£ 9.95
Barker, Alan	Making Meetings Work	1993	£ 8.95
Brollo, Paul	The Grammar Workbook	1999	£15.99
Cammock-Elliott, Bede	Get a Life: A success guide for young people	1997	£ 9.99
Clarke, Jane	Office Politics: A survival guide	1999	£10.99
Forrest, Andrew	Fifty Ways to Personal Development	1995	£ 6.95
Forrest, Andrew	5 Way Management	1997	£12.95
James, Judi	People Talk	1997	£ 9.95
	Body Talk	1995	£ 9.95
	Sex at Work	1998	£ 8.99
Turner, David	Liberating Leadership	1998	£14.99

All these books are published by The Industrial Society. Contact the Sales Unit on 0121 410 3040 for further details of these and other Industrial Society publications.